The Ninja Foodi Pressure Cooker Cookbook

Your Expert Guide to Air Fry, Pressure Cook and Multi-Cooker Recipes for Living and Eating Well Every Day

Keith Moore

Table of contents

Introduction...10

CHAPTER 1: NINJA FOODI PRESSURE COOKER BASICS 12

   Benefits of the Ninja Foodi Pressure Cooker 15

   Ninja Foodi Pressure Cooker, use and tips 17

CHAPTER 2: BREAKFAST RECIPES 18

   Recipe 1: French toast 19

   Recipe 2: Monkey Bread 20

   Recipe 3: Breakfast Granola 22

   Recipe 4: Mushroom Sausage Breakfast 24

   Recipe 5: Air Fryer Ninja Foodi Ground Sausage Breakfast 26

   Recipe 6: Ham breakfast with cheese 28

   Recipe 7: Egg Bites 30

   Recipe 8: Chocolate Chip Pancake 32

   Recipe 9: Ninja Foodi Pumpkin Oatmeal 34

   Recipe 10: Breakfast Pizza 36

   Recipe 11: Chocolate Oatmeal 38

   Recipe 12: Scotch Eggs 40

   Recipe 13: Deviled Eggs 42

   Recipe 14: Ninja Foodi Breakfast Dates Pudding 43

   Recipe 15: Ninja Foodi Omelette 45

   Recipe 16: Thai-Style Omelette 47

   Recipe 17: Breakfast Quiche 49

   Recipe 18: Oatmeal Muffins 51

   Recipe 19: Bacon Egg Cheese Roll 53

   Recipe 20: Quinoa Breakfast Bowl 55

   Recipe 21: Ninja Foodi Banana Porridge 56

   Recipe 22: Scrambled Eggs 57

CHAPTER 3: SNACKS AND APPETIZER RECIPES...................................59

   Recipe 23: Jalapeño peppers 60

Recipe 24: Ninja Fried Ravioli 61
Recipe 25: Egg plant Fries 62
Recipe 26: Garlic Fried Potatoes.. 64
Recipe 27: Zucchini Fries 66
Recipe 28: Ninja Fried Onion Rings.. 68
Recipe 29: Ninja Foodi Vegetable Appetizer 70
Recipe 30: Ninja Foodi Corn Dogs 72
Recipe 31: Fried Kale... 74
Recipe 32: Ninja Foodi Falafel 75
Recipe 33: Crispy Wontons 77
Recipe 34: Mini Cheese and salami Pizzas.. 79
Recipe 35: Cheese Chips 81
Recipe 36: Ninja Foodi Pretzels... 82
Recipe 37: French Sticks 84
Recipe 38: Sausage balls 86
Recipe 39: Chicken Bites 87
Recipe 40: Stuffed Potatoes 88
Recipe 41: Cauliflower bites 90
Recipe 42: Samosa 92
Recipe 43: Ninja Foodi Chicken Enchiladas 94
Recipe 44: Stuffed Peppers 96

CHAPTER 4: VEGETABLE RECIPES 98

Recipe 45: Vegetable Ratatouille... 99
Recipe 46: Ninja Foodi Cooked Vegetables 101
Recipe 47: Ninja Foodi Steamed Broccoli... 102
Recipe 48: Potato with bacon... 104
Recipe 49: Ninja Foodi Beets 106
Recipe 50: Ninja Foodi Pinto Beans 107
Recipe 51: Vegetables Pie.. 108
Recipe 52: Ninja Foodi Green Beans 110
Recipe 53: Garlicky Tomatoes 111
Recipe 54: Couscous with chickpeas 113
Recipe 55: Egg and Vegetables Salad.. 115

CHAPTER 5: FISH AND SEAFOOD RECIPES 117

Recipe 56: Ninja Foodi Fish and Chips ... 118
Recipe 57: Pomfret Fish Fry ... 120
Recipe 58: Tandoori Fish ... 122
Recipe 59: Pecan Coated, Honey-Glazed Salmon ... 124
Recipe 60: Panko Crusted Halibut ... 126
Recipe 61: Prawn Curry ... 128
Recipe 62: Ninja Foodi fried Air Fried Shrimp ... 130
Recipe 63: Bacon Wrapped shrimps ... 132
Recipe 64: Octopus Chili ... 134
Recipe 65: Rooly Poly Chinese-Style Fish ... 136
Recipe 66: Mahi Mahi Fish with Iceberg Leaves ... 137
Recipe 67: Ninja Foodi Fish and Grits ... 139
Recipe 68: Ninja Foodi Fried Catfish ... 141
Recipe 69: Crab Cakes ... 143
Recipe 70: Corn and Mussels Ninja Foodi Casserole ... 145
Recipe 71: Spicy Shrimp Fajitas ... 147
Recipe 72: Ninja Foodi Halibut Sitka ... 148
Recipe 73: Cedar Planked Salmon ... 149
Recipe 74: Crab Leg Ninja Foodi Pot ... 151
Recipe 75: Bang Bang Shrimp ... 153
Recipe 76: Ninja Foodi Panko Crusted Cod with Quinoa ... 155
Recipe 77: Ninja Foodi Mackerels ... 157

CHAPTER 6: POULTRY RECIPES ... 158

Recipe 78: Southern-style chicken ... 159

Recipe 79: Stuffed Chicken with Tomato Sauce ... 161
Recipe 80: Asian-Style Chicken ... 163
Recipe 81: Broccoli with Sesame Chicken ... 165
Recipe 82: Chicken with Garlic and Mushrooms ... 167
Recipe 83: Chicken Breast with mustard and herbs ... 169
Recipe 84: Honey-Glazed Chicken wings ... 171
Recipe 85: Chicken Nuggets with Mayonnaise ... 173
Recipe 86: Chicken Pakora ... 174
Recipe 87: Cashew Chicken ... 176
Recipe 88: Spicy Buffalo Chicken ... 177
Recipe 89: Chicken with Prunes and Olives ... 179

Recipe 90: Chicken Chutney 181
Recipe 91: Chicken Potato Nests 183
Recipe 92: Chicken Liver and cauliflower Bites 185
Recipe 93: Chicken Salad 187
Recipe 94: Chicken Quinoa Salad 189
Recipe 95: Ninja Foodi Chicken casserole 191
Recipe 96: Greek-Style CHICKEN 193
Recipe 97: Chicken Chettinad 195
Recipe 98: Ninja Foodi Whole Turkey 197
Recipe 99: Chicken Kebabs 199
Recipe 100: Chicken Patties 201
CONCLUSION 202

© Copyright 2020 By Keith Moore All Right Reserved.

In no way it is legal to reproduce, duplicate, or transmit any part of this document by other electronic means or printed format. Any recording of this publication is strictly prohibited, and any storage of this material is not allowed unless with a written permission from the publisher. All rights reserved.

The information provided herein is stated to be truthful and consistent, in that any liability, regarding inattention or otherwise, by any use or abuse of any policies, processes, or directions contained within is the solitary and complete responsibility of the recipient reader. Under no circumstances will any legal liability or blame be held against the publisher for any reparation, damages, or monetary loss due to the information herein, either directly or indirectly.

Legal Notice:

This book is copyright protected. This is only for personal use. You cannot amend, distribute, sell, use, quote or paraphrase any part or the content within this book without the consent of the author or copyright owner. Legal action will be pursued if it is breached

DISCLAIMER NOTICE:

Please only read the information contained within this document is for educational purposes only. Every attempt has been made to provide accurate, up to date, complete and reliable information. No warranties of any kind are expressed or implied. Readers acknowledge that the author is not engaged in the rendering of legal, financial, medical or professional advice.

By reading this document, the reader agrees that under no circumstances are we responsible for any losses, direct or indirect, which are incurred as a result of the use of information contained in this document, including but not limited to errors, omissions, or any inaccuracies

Introduction

If you want to offer your family a delicious meal after a busy day or during the weekend, but at the same time, you want to spend time with them and enjoy your family gatherings and special occasions, you have come to the right place. Indeed, this is the best book to start from and thanks to it; you will be able to offer your family the meals they have been starving for a long a time

What you are about to experience us a unique cooking method that has never been experienced by people you have known before; it is a unique cooking method that you will get addicted to once you try it. The new technology of Ninja Pressure cookers will offer you the speed of fast conventional pressure cookers and the revolutionary crispiness air fryers at the same time.

The revolutionary technology Ninja pressure cookers offer allows, not only cooking your ingredients in a short time; but gives all your meals a great crispiness and a golden cooking touch that you dream of. So if you don't want to make your family wait any longer and you are ready to jump into your kitchen; don't wait anymore; because the Ninja Instant Cooker's pressure cooking ability will help you prepare flavorful meals right on time and the taste will be imaginary.

Ninja Pressure cookers use pressurized steam allowing steam to infuse extra moisture and flavor to your ingredients cooking it from the inside out and offering you a masterful dish you never imagined you can perfect. So, we can say that Ninja Pressure cookers start with a tender taste of the pressure cookers and ends with the crispiness of Air Fryers offering you a heavenly taste and extraordinary tender and crispy results at the same time. And do you know what the best part of using Ninja Pressure cookers is; it is that there is more than a single way to let you enjoy the tender crispiness you have been looking for.

Besides, with Nina Pressure cookers; you can start by using ingredients that are fresh or frozen. And if you are wondering what you can cook in Ninja Pressure cookers, don't worry, because you can cook almost everything starting with veggies, chicken, fish and different types of meals and dishes. Surprisingly enough, you can prepare stews, soups and chilies in Ninja Pressure Cookers.

And whether you have heard about the Ninja Foodi Pressure cooker while you have been searching for air fryers or pressure cookers, rest assured because you have "landed" on the right cooking appliance that will change all your previous perceptions and conceptions you have about the entire culinary experience. But if this is the first time you hear about Ninja Foodi Pressure Cookers, and you are not sure if it does live up to its name; then it is the right time to wipe all your doubts and dive into one of the most beneficial and pleasant cooking experiences that you can ever have.

So what's the Ninja Foodi Pressure cooker? Everyone knows how the Instant Pots and Air Fryers claim to be the number one cooking appliances that suit all your culinary uses; it is just the cooking appliance each of us needs. And this isn't all; the Ninja Foodi Pressure Cooker takes the use of Ninja foodi Pressure Cooker a step further by combining the power of air fryers to that of Instant Pots.

The Ninja Foodi Pressure Cooker can slow cook, pressure cook; steam; sauté and air fry. Besides, Nina Foodi Pressure Cookers also display a Tender crisp technology that is basically a combination of air frying and Pressure cooking; admittedly, a conventional Instant Pot can't do that. And people, who have used the revolutionary cooking appliance Ninja Foodi Pressure Cooker, agree on the fact that this cooking appliance stands out from the rest of the cooking appliances.

Owning a Foodi Ninja Pressure cooker is supposed to save your money, time and even space in the kitchen as it will replace three separate important cooking appliances that you may have used simultaneously to get the taste you are looking for. And while it is true that Ninja Foodi Pressure cooker will take more space in the kitchen than Air Fryers and Instant Pots; but overall, using this cooking appliance will reduce the clutter.

So, if you are passionate about cooking and the culinary world and you want to learn more about the use of the Foodi Ninja Pressure Cooker; this cook book is a great place to start from. And whether you are a beginner or a professional cook, and wherever you live, you will always find something for you in this cookbook; so what are you waiting for to get started and get your own copy of this cookbook?

And before jumping right to the world of Ninja Foodi pressure cooking, congratulations; you have made a great choice in purchasing this cooking appliance.

CHAPTER 1: NINJA FOODI PRESSURE COOKER BASICS

If you are not exactly sure if you want to purchase a Ninja Foodi Pressure Cooker or not and you want to know more about the use and the basics of this revolutionary cooking appliance and all its features; here is a brief description of what it does exactly. Indeed, a Ninja Foodi with TenderCrisp technology is considered as an electric cooking appliance that usually functions as a cooker that has a multi-use.

Ninja Foodi Pressure Cooker has two main features that are air fryer and pressure cooker; yet it also does much more than these two uses. And here are the main features of any Ninja Foodi pressure cooker. And the following features are used usually with the pressure cooking lid on:

1. Slow Cook:

This function works like a slow cooker would and it can be set both high or Low. You can also customize the slow cooking time up to about 12 hours. And when using this feature, you should set the black valve right on top; but make sure it is set to vent and not to seal position.

2. Pressure Cooker:

The pressure cooking function may be set to Hi or Low; besides you can also customize the time that you need and you want your food to about 4 hours. And when using the pressure cooking function, you should turn the black valve right on top of the Ninja Foodi to Seal.

3. Steam:

There is no special temperature adjustment that you need to adhere to when using the setting steam. You can for example, adjust the time to about 30 minutes and when using this feature; it is also important to make sure that the black valve on the top is set to vent, instead of seal.

4. Sear/Sauté:

This feature is used with or without a lid on the Ninja Foodi. And this feature has a multitude of temperature settings; Hi; Med, Med-Hi, Med-Low and Low. But with this feature, you don't have the ability to set the time and it will rather stay on the function off. You can also use the pressure lid with the function sauté; but it is recommended to use the sear/sauté without a lid so that you can keep an eye on your food instantly and easily.

5. Air Crisp with TenderCrisp Technology:

This Air Crisp function usually has temperature settings between about 300° F to about 400° F. And the following features are usually used with the crisping lid on. But you can also customize the time for about 1 hour.

6. **Bake Roast feature:**

The bake/roast feature usually displays temperature settings from temperatures of about 250° F up to 400° F and you can also customize the time up to about 4 hours.

7. The function broil: This function Broil does not usually have a specific temperature adjustment; it is usually either on or off. You can adjust the time up to about 30 minutes.
8. **Dehydration:**

This feature is only used on certain brands of Ninja Foodi pressure cookers and it is only used with the crisping lid on. And the dehydration function allows adjusting the temperature from about 105°F to 195°F. You can also adjust the time from about 15 minutes to 12 hours.

Benefits of the Ninja Foodi Pressure Cooker

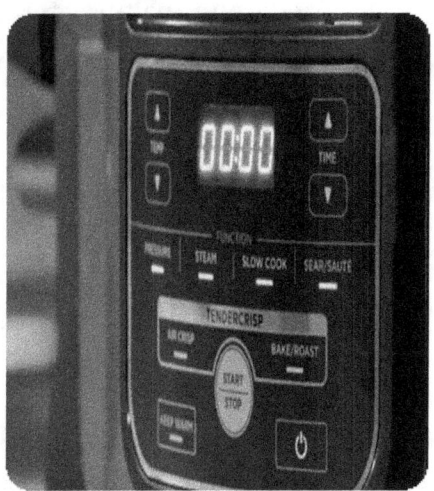

The Ninja Foodi Pressure Cooker is very easy to use and to function. This cooking appliance works in a similar way to the Air Fryer, Instant Pots and other cooking appliances and electric pressure cookers. But before using this revolutionary cooking appliance Ninja Foodi pressure cooker, you should first know the major basics, using tips and most importantly the benefits of using Ninja Pressure cookers.

1. Ninja Foodi Pressure Cookers are easy to use and doesn't cause any confusion when using it. The features of Ninja Pressure cookers are clear and will fit in any place or corner in your kitchen. And whether you want to cook a savory dish or a dessert, this cooking appliance makes a perfect choice for you.

2. Ninja Foodi Pressure Cookers will help you save the space of two cooking appliances, the air fryer and Instant Pot. And you can pressure cook anything immediately and get the crispy taste you are looking for in no time. This cooking method works very well with whole chickens, because it needs to be cooked tender; then get the crispy taste you want. And possessing this cooking appliance; you don't need to bring your chicken to a broiler to get the crispiness you are looking for.

3. The user interface of Ninja Foodi Pressure Cookers is very simple and easy to use with a clean design and the buttons are easy to understand its functions. With this kitchen appliance, you can cook two things, just at once.

4. Ninja Foodi Pressure Cookers can save your time; indeed, with the help of this kitchen appliance, you can cook a healthy and delicious meal in a short time without the need to use many cooking appliances. Besides, this kitchen cookware is characterized by a large cooking capacity.

5. All of the pieces that come with the Ninja Foodi are easy to clean.

6. Ninja Foodi Pressure Cookers come with accessories that are easy to use and that can make the baking experience easier.

7. The pot of the Ninja Foodi is a bit wider and shorter than conventional Instant Pot; so you have more surfaces for a better browning process. This cooking appliance is great for desserts; and for making individual portions in special, like muffins.

8. Ninja Foodi heats up quicker than other cooking appliances; and it reaches up full pressure within four to six minutes for non-frozen recipes.

9. The sealing valve is easy to secure it in place and very little quantity of steam is released in the air.

10. A major benefit of using Ninja Foodi over many other cooking appliances is, for example that you can't open the oven to turn the fries multiples times while with the Ninja Foodi, you can shake the fries around half-way through the cooking process to help cook evenly.

➤ *Note:*

Ninja Foodi Pressure Cooker is a multicooker, an air fryer and it has a built-in crisping element that is easy-to use and that can save your time and offer you the crispy taste you have been looking for a long time.

Ninja Foodi Pressure Cooker, use and tips

More and more people are choosing Ninja Foodi Pressure Cooker as their primal cooking appliance for the various benefits it offers. Indeed, between the years 2010 and 2017, the sales of Pressure cookers in general, rose by a percentage that hit the roof of more than 32 percent. And today, we can say that electric pressure cookers are becoming more popular just as popular as small appliances, like microwaves and ovens and microwaves. But before using any cooking appliance in general, especially an appliance like the Ninja Foodie Pressure Cookers, there are some tips and basics you should know and that will help you master use this appliance.

1. The Ninja Foodi TenderCrisp Pressure Cooker is known for being a heavy and big cooking machine, so you will need to have a kind of big space to use it.

2. The crisping lid of the Ninja Foodi Pressure Cooker is not removable and is hinged. So you need room to open the lid while you are using Ninja Foodi pressure cookers. And the attached air fryer lid means that you can't cook with the Ninja Foodi over a counter under your cabinets.

3. The electrical cord of Ninja Foodi Pressure Cookers is generally about 33inches in length; so you need to be close to an electric outlet to be able to use it.

4. The pressure release valve on the Foodi is usually short and it is more difficult to maneuver in comparison to that of the Instant Pot without bringing into contact with the steam.

5. Hot air comes out from the back of the cooking appliance as it works as air frying, so you need to make sure to place it away from your cabinets and walls.

6. Many accessories that fit conventional 6-quart pressure cookers will be considered tall to be used in the Ninja Foodi.

7. The beep you will hear at the end is a beep that is not loud, but it is not adjustable.

CHAPTER 2: BREAKFAST RECIPES

Recipe 1: French toast

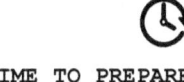
TIME TO PREPARE
5 minutes

COOK TIME
20 minutes

SERVING
4 People

Ingredients

- 2 packs of grands cinnamon rolls
- 4 Large eggs
- 1 Tablespoon of vanilla
- 2 Tablespoon of milk
- 1 Tablespoon of cinnamon

Instructions

1. Start by whisking all together the eggs, the milk and the vanilla
2. Now, open the grands cinnamon rolls and just quarter each dough and place the icing aside aside
3. Spray the insert to the Ninja foodi with cooking oil or Pam.
4. Place the dough in the pan; then pour over the mixture of the egg.
5. Turn the Ninja Foodi on bake for about 350°F and close the air fry lid
6. Bake for about 20 minutes.
7. Top with the Syrup or the icing from the rolls
8. Serve and enjoy your breakfast!

Nutrition Information

Calories: 161, Fat: 6g, Carbohydrates: 20g, Dietary Fiber: 1 g, Protein: 6g

Recipe 2: Monkey Bread

TIME TO PREPARE
10 minutes

COOK TIME
18 Minutes

SERVING
4 People

Ingredients

- 2 Cans of cinnamon rolls, cut into about 8 pieces each
- 1 Large apple, cut into pieces of about ¼ inch to ½ inch each.
- ¼ cup of white sugar
- ¼ cup of brown sugar
- ¼ cup of chopped walnuts
- ¼ cup of chopped pecans
- ¼ cup of heath chips
- cinnamon roll icing
- 1 Cup of water
- Non-Stick Cooking Spray

Instructions

1. Cut the canned cinnamon rolls into about 8 pieces each.
2. In a large bowl; combine the cinnamon rolls with the sugar, the pecans, the walnuts, the chips and the apples.
3. Mix all your ingredients until the biscuits are perfectly coated; make sure to separate the biscuit pieces of each other and that they are not clumped together
4. Spray the mini Bundt pan with a non stick cooking spray.
5. Fill the mini Bundt pan with the biscuit mixture; then press down very well until the mixture perfectly fits in the pan.
6. Pour in 1 cup of water into the Ninja Foodi.
7. Place the mini b=Bundt pan into your Ninja Foodi after using a sling or just place on the trivet.
8. Close the "pressure cooking" lid and make sure to

move the valve to "seal" position.
9. Turn the Ninja Foodi "on" and choose the "pressure cooking" setting; then set the time to about 18 minutes.
10. Push the button "start." And once the timer beeps; do a natural releasing pressure for about 4 minutes; then quick release the remaining pressure.
11. Open the lid of the Ninja Foodi; then remove the mini bundt pan from the Ninja Foodi and let cool for about 5 to 10 minutes.
12. Once perfectly cooled, flip the Bundt pan to a serving plate and lift the Bundt pan away from the monkey bread.
13. Mix the melted butter with the brown sugar together very well; then pour over the Caramel Apple Monkey Bread.
14. Drizzle the canned frosting over the monkey bread.
15. Serve and enjoy your breakfast!

Nutrition Information

Calories: 200, Fat: 10g, Carbohydrates: 26g, Dietary Fiber: 1 g, Protein: 3g

Recipe 3: Breakfast Granola

TIME TO PREPARE
5 minutes

COOK TIME
15 Minutes

SERVING
4 People

Ingredients

- 3 Cups of rolled oats
- ½ Cup of shredded coconut
- ½ cup of coconut smiles
- ½ cup of sunflower seeds
- ½ cup of pumpkin seeds
- 1 cup of dried fruits
- ½ Cup of coconut oil
- ½ Cup of seed, butter or soy
- ½ cup of maple syrup
- ½ tsp of salt
- 1 tsp of cinnamon

Instructions

1. In a large bowl; place the coconut, the oats, the coconut smiles, the sunflower seeds, the pumpkin seeds, and the cinnamon to a large bowl and mix very well.
2. Add the coconut oil, the seed butter, the maple syrup, and the salt to a glass bowl and microwave for about 30 to 60 seconds until everything is melted.
3. Stir your ingredients very well; then pour the liquid mixture over the dry ingredients and stir very well
4. Dump the mixture over a parchment paper covered sheet pan; then spread evenly making sure to press down a little bit
5. Press the button function, Air Fryer and toss the ingredients in your Ninja Foodi
6. Air Fry for about 15 minutes at a temperature of about 350°F
7. Add the dried fruit; then let cool on a pan
8. Transfer to an airtight container
9. Enjoy your granola!

Nutrition Information

Calories: 140, Fat: 9g, Carbohydrates: 14g, Dietary Fiber: 3 g, Protein: 3 g

Recipe 4: Mushroom Sausage Breakfast

TIME TO PREPARE
8 minutes

COOK TIME
11 minutes

SERVING
3 People

Ingredients

- ¾ cup of diced onion
- 1 tbsp of olive oil
- 5 Sliced mushrooms
- 8 Scrambled eggs
- ¼ Cup of cream of mushroom soup
- ½ tsp of garlic salt
- ¾ Cup of shredded cheese
- ½ lb of spicy ground sausage
- 1 Diced chive

Instructions

1. Turn on your Ninja Foodi; then press the setting function sauté.
2. Add the olive oil, the diced onions, and the ground sausage, bacon, spicy
3. Cook until about halfway done; then add in the sliced mushrooms and cook until the sausage becomes no longer pink
4. Press the setting button stop on the machine
5. In a large bowl; scramble the eggs; then pour into the Ninja Foodi with the meat.
6. Sprinkle in the garlic salt, about ½ cup of the shredded cheese; then add in ¼ cup of cream of mushroom soup or alfredo sauce
7. Stir your ingredients very well; then close the air fryer lid
8. Press the air crisp button and set the temperature at about 390°F for about 6 minutes
9. Lift the lid and stir so the uncooked egg on bottom is perfectly circulated to make sure everything is cooked thoroughly.
10. Close the lid of your Ninja Foodi again and set to air

crisp, at a temperature of about 390°F degrees for an additional 4 to 5 minutes.
11. Serve and enjoy your omelette with cheese on top and with a sprinkle of chives!

Nutrition Information

Calories: 294, Fat: 22g, Carbohydrates: 3g, Dietary Fiber: 1 g, Protein: 17g

Recipe 5: Air Fryer Ninja Foodi Ground Sausage Breakfast

TIME TO PREPARE
6 minutes

COOK TIME
15 Minutes

SERVING
3-4 People

Ingredients

- 1 lb of Ground Sausage
- ¼ Cup of Diced White Onion
- 1 Diced of Green Bell Pepper
- 8 Beaten Whole Eggs
- ½ Cup of shredded Colby Jack Cheese
- 1 Teaspoon of Fennel Seed
- ½ Teaspoon of Garlic Salt

Instructions

1. Use the sauté function of your Ninja Foodi; then brown the sausage in the pot of the foodi
2. Add the onion and the pepper and cook with the ground sausage until the veggies are very well cooked
3. Using the Air Fryer pan, spray with a non-stick cooking spray; then put the ground sausage mixture into the bottom and top with the cheese evenly
4. Pour the beaten eggs evenly on top of the cheese and the sausage.
5. Add the fennel seed and the garlic salt evenly on top of the eggs.
6. Put the rack in a low position into the Ninja Foodi; then place the pan right on top
7. Set your Ninja Foodi to Air Crisp for about 15 minutes at about 390°F
8. Carefully remove from the Ninja Foodi and serve!

Nutrition Information

Calories: 282, Fat: 23g, Carbohydrates: 3g, Dietary Fiber: 2g, Protein: 15g

Recipe 6: Ham breakfast with cheese

TIME TO PREPARE
10 minutes

COOK TIME
8 Hours

SERVING
4 People

Ingredients

- 2 Tbsp of salted butter
- 1 Diced onion
- 1 Pound of chopped potatoes
- 1 Pound of chopped ham
- 11 to 12 Large eggs
- 1 Cup of heavy whipping cream
- 16 ounces of grated cheddar cheese

Instructions

1. Chop the onion into about ½ inch dice.
2. Turn on your Ninja Foodi on the function High Sear/Saute.
3. Add the butter and the onions and sauté for about 5 minutes.
4. While the onions are being sautéed, cut the potatoes into pieces; then add to the pot
5. Crack the eggs in a large mixing bowl and whisk with Immersion blender
6. Chop the ham into pieces of about 1 inch each
7. Turn off your Ninja Foodie; then dump the eggs and the heavy cream
8. Stir very well to combine
9. Place the pressure lid on; then turn the seal to vent and set the slow cooker function to low for about 8 hours
10. Serve with the remaining quantity of cheddar cheese and broil for about 4 minutes
11. Serve and enjoy your breakfast!

Nutrition Information

Calories: 523, Fat: 40g, Carbohydrates: 8g, Dietary Fiber: 1 g, Protein: 31g

Recipe 7: Egg Bites

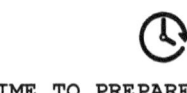

TIME TO PREPARE
10 minutes

COOK TIME
17 Minutes

SERVING
5-6 People

Ingredients

- 4 to 5 slices of bacon
- ½ cup of lite coconut milk or of regular milk canned
- 1 cup of Spinach cut up
- 6 Large eggs

Instructions

1. Start by cooking the bacon in your Ninja Foodi and to do that, use the Air crisper basket; then place the bacon slices inside the basket and air crisp for about 10 minutes at a temperature of about 400°F
2. Remove the crisping basket and set it aside; then crack about 6 eggs and add the bacon grease; the spinach and the coconut milk
3. Season with the salt and the pepper to taste and mix very well
4. Set the mold on the trivet; then pour each mold evenly of the prepared mixture.
5. Set the trivet and the mold in your Ninja Foodi; then lower the crisping lid and set at about 325°F for about 17 minutes
6. Remove; then set to cool
7. Serve and enjoy your breakfast!

Nutrition Information

Calories: 170, Fat: 7g, Carbohydrates: 13g, Dietary Fiber: 1 g, Protein: 13g

Recipe 8: Chocolate Chip Pancake

TIME TO PREPARE
9 minutes

COOK TIME
10 Minutes

SERVING
4 People

Ingredients

- 3Cups of self-Raising flour
- 1 tsp of baking powder
- 3 tbsp of caster sugar
- 2 Medium eggs
- 300ml of whole milk
- 2 Cups of milk chocolate chips
- Butter, for frying
- whipped cream to serve

Instructions

1. In a bowl; crack the eggs; then add the caster sugar; the milk and the chocolate chips and mix very well or whisk until you get a thick mixture
2. Prepare a 3 cup Bundt pan; and lightly spray its bottom with non stick spray; then pour the batter into the pan
3. Pour 1 cup of water to the Nina Foodi Pot and place the pan over a trivet rack; then lower down into the pot
4. Set up the timer for about 10 minutes and the pressure to High Manual
5. Quick release the pressure when the cooking pressure is over
6. Lower the Air Crisp lid and set on the temperature of about 390°F for about 5 minutes
7. Remove the pancake from the pot and let cool for several minutes; then drizzle with the golden syrup
8. Serve and enjoy your breakfast pancakes!

Nutrition Information

Calories: 139, Fat: 7g, Carbohydrates: 16g, Dietary Fiber: 0.8 g, Protein: 3.4g

Recipe 9: Ninja Foodi Pumpkin Oatmeal

TIME TO PREPARE
7 minutes

COOK TIME
12 Minutes

SERVING
3 People

Ingredients

- 3 Cups of Old Fashioned Oats or Gluten-Free Old Fashioned Oats
- ¼ Cup of Brown Sugar
- ¼ Tsp of Baking Powder
- 1 Tsp of salt
- 1 Teaspoon of Cinnamon
- 2 Tsp of Pumpkin Pie Spice
- 1 Tsp of Nutmeg
- 2 Large eggs
- 1 and ½ cups of Milk
- 1 Cup of Pumpkin Pure

Instructions

1. Combine all your ingredients in a large mixing bowl; then spray the pot of the Ninja Foodi with cooking spray; like grapeseed oil
2. Spread the oatmeal into the bottom of your Ninjja Foodi in an even way
3. Close the lid that is on your Foodi.
4. Use the button function "Bake" and set to a temperature of about 325°F for about 30 minutes.
5. Serve your oatmeal with cool or warm milk!

Nutrition Information

Calories: 212, Fat: 5g, Carbohydrates: 35g, Dietary Fiber: 5 g, Protein: 8g

Recipe 10: Breakfast Pizza

TIME TO PREPARE
6 minutes

COOK TIME
5 Minutes

SERVING
4 People

Ingredients

- 1 Tube of commercially prepared pizza dough
- ½ cup of butter
- 1 tsp of garlic
- 1 Sprinkle of fresh parsley
- 2 Cup of shredded Mozzarella cheese

Instructions

1. Open the pizza dough and unroll it; then check for any cracks or holes
2. Reroll your dough and roll it on its long side
3. Cut the rolls into slices of about 1 inch each and faltten into about 6" of diameter
4. Combine the butter with the garlic, and the herbs together.
5. Brush the butter and garlic on top of the dough; then place on the Foodi rack and air crisp the dough for about 4 to 5 minutes
6. Flip and brush the dough again with butter; then do the air fry for the other side
7. Sprinkle some cheese over the top of the brad and air fry for a few minutes
8. Add any toppings of your choice
9. Serve and enjoy your breakfast pizza

Nutrition Information

Calories: 182, Fat: 17g, Carbohydrates: 5g, Dietary Fiber: 0 g, Protein: 6g

Recipe 11: Chocolate Oatmeal

TIME TO PREPARE
5 minutes

COOK TIME
5 Minutes

SERVING
3 People

Ingredients

- 2 cups of quick oats
- 4 cups of chocolate almond milk
- ½ cup of chocolate chips

Instructions

1. Spray the inside of an oven safe dish with non stick cooking spray.
2. Add in the quick oats and the chocolate almond milk into the bowl and stir very well
3. Add in 1 ½ cups of water into the bottom of the Ninja Foodie pot and lower the trivet down with the filled bowl on top.
4. Put the lid of the Ninja Foodi on and pressure cook after choosing the setting function "Pressure cook"; then cover with the lid and close the steam valve
5. Set for pressure at high, for about 5 minutes.
6. Do a quick pressure release when the time is up
7. Stir; then serve with the chocolate chips and strawberries of over the top
8. Enjoy your breakfast!

Nutrition Information

Calories: 296, Fat: 11g, Carbohydrates: 43g, Dietary Fiber: 5 g, Protein: 7g

Recipe 12: Scotch Eggs

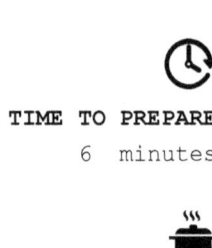

TIME TO PREPARE
6 minutes

COOK TIME
10 Minutes

SERVING
7 People

Ingredients

- 7 Large eggs
- 1 kb of ground sausage Jimmy deans breakfast
- HP sauce
- 2 Tablespoons of Non-stick butter spray

Instructions

1. Start by spraying an egg bite mold lightly with non-stick butter spray.
2. With the help of a table spoon, scoop the sausage and form it around the bottom of your mold; make sure to spread it evenly and in a firm way
3. Crack the egg; then drop on top of the sausage into the cavity of the mold.
4. Pour 1 cup of water inside your Ninja Foodi; then set on the mold over a trivet with handles
5. Lower down the trivet in the foodi; then set the pressure to High for about 12 minutes
6. Do a quick release pressure method to release the steam; then when the pin drops remove the lid and lower down the Air Crisp lid an set on about 350°F for an additional 4 to 5 minutes
7. Remove from the Pot and set to cool for about 5 minutes. Pop the Scotch eggs and get the sauce out of the pot
8. Serve and enjoy your breakfast!

Nutrition Information

Calories: 300, Fat: 21g, Carbohydrates: 16g, Dietary Fiber: 0g, Protein: 12g

Recipe 13: Deviled Eggs

TIME TO PREPARE
7 minutes

COOK TIME
5 Minutes

SERVING
12 People

Ingredients

- 12 hard, cooked, peeled and cut peeled and cooked eggs, peeled and cut lengthwise
- 4 Tablespoon of mayonnaise
- 2 Tablespoon of sweet pickle juice
- 4 Teaspoons of spicy brown mustard
- 1 Pinch of salt and 1 pinch of pepper to taste

Instructions

1. Pour 1 cup of water into your Ninja Foodi Pressure cooker pot.
2. Place the eggs in the bottom of your Instant pot; then lock the lid.
3. Cook on a High pressure for about 5 minutes with a 5-minute natural release.
4. Let the eggs cool in an ice bath for about 5 minutes
5. Peel the eggs and cut it in a lengthwise way
6. Using a food processor or a mixer; then mix the egg yolks with the mayonnaise, the pickle juice, the mustard, the salt and the pepper until it becomes smooth.
7. Pipe the yolk mixture into each of the egg whites.
8. Lay small pieces of chives on top; then serve and enjoy your breakfast!

Nutrition Information

Calories: 116, Fat: 8g, Carbohydrates: 3g, Dietary Fiber: 0g, Protein: 6g

Recipe 14: Ninja Foodi Breakfast Dates Pudding

TIME TO PREPARE
12 minutes

COOK TIME
55 Minutes

SERVING
4 People

Ingredients

- 2 Cups of chopped pitted dates
- 150ml of hot water
- 1 Teaspoon of bicarbonate of soda
- 1 Cup of softened unsalted butter
- ½ Cup of dark muscovado sugar
- 1 large beaten egg
- 1 ½ Cups of self raising flour
- 1 teaspoon of ground ginger

For The Sauce

- 1 ½ cups of unsalted butter
- 1 Cup of dark muscovado sugar
- 200ml of double cream
- 1 Pinch of sea salt

Instructions

1. Grease the Multi-Purpose Pan of your Ninja Foodi and set it aside
2. Preheat your Ninja Foodi unit by selecting the setting function BAKE/ROAST
3. Set the temperature to about 350°F and the time to about 5 minutes
4. Select the START/STOP; then place the dates into hot water with the bicarbonate of soda and soak for about 10 minutes.
5. When the dates become soft, puree it into a food processor and set it aside.
6. Meanwhile, combine the butter and the sugar with a hand mixer or a stand mixer on a medium high speed
7. Add in the eggs and incorporate very well with the help of a rubber spatula
8. Add in the flour; the ginger and 1 pinch of salt
9. Add in the dates and mix your ingredients very well
10. Pour the mixture into the pan and smooth it with a spatula
11. Place the pan over the reversible rack and ake sure the rack is in lower position

- Vanilla ice cream

12. Place the rack with the pan in the pot
13. Close the crisping lid; then select the BAKE/ROAST; then set the temperature to about 345°F and set the time to about 35 minutes.
14. Select the START/STOP to begin the cooking process and bake for about 5 to 10 additional minutes for perfect cooking; but make sure to cover with aluminum foil to avoid any risk of burning
15. When the cooking process is complete; remove and set it aside while making your sauce.
16. Select the SEAR/SAUTÉ and set to HI; then select the START/STOP to start.
17. Add in the butter and the sugar and whisk; then add in the cream and cook for 1 additional 1 minute
18. Add in the salt and stir; then press the START/STOP button and carefully pour the sauce in a jug
19. Serve and enjoy your pudding with a scoop of vanilla ice cream!

Nutrition Information

Calories: 210, Fat: 11g, Carbohydrates: 22g, Dietary Fiber: 0g, Protein: 6g

Recipe 15: Ninja Foodi Omelette

TIME TO PREPARE
5 minutes

COOK TIME
6 Minutes

SERVING
3 People

Ingredients

- 2 Tablespoons of butter
- ½ Medium, finely chopped onion
- 2 Garlic cloves
- 1 Cup of steel cut oats
- 1 Can of about 14 ounces can of chicken broth
- ½ Cup of water
- 3 Sprigs of fresh thyme
- ¼ Teaspoon of salt
- 2 Tablespoons of olive oil
- 8 Oz of sliced Crimini mushrooms
- ½ Cup of finely grated smoked gouda
- 1 Pinch of salt and 1 pinch of freshly

Instructions

1. Start by whisking your eggs, the cheese, the milk, the salt and the pepper all together in a large bowl then, blend them well.
2. Sprit your pan with a non-stick cooking spray
3. Now, put the meat in the "Air and Crisp" steam basket of your Air Fryer.
4. Pour the mixture of the eggs you obtained in the pan and add the asparagus to the egg mixture and place them all together in the pan.
5. Carefully, place your pan on the rack and slowly slide the basket into the Ninja Foodi Air Fryer.
6. Use the Air Crisp setting and set the temperature up to 320° F and the time to 6 minutes.
7. Now, halfway the cooking time; shake your basket so that you can move your eggs a little bit around.
8. When the omelette is ready you will notice it is light and looks fluffy.
9. Serve and enjoy your Omelette

ground pepper

Nutrition Information

Calories: 154, Fat: 12g, Carbohydrates: 0.6g, Dietary Fiber: 0g, Protein: 11g

Recipe 16: Thai-Style Omelette

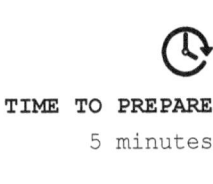

TIME TO PREPARE
5 minutes

COOK TIME
5 Minutes

SERVING
3 People

Ingredients

- 4 large eggs
- 1-3 tbsp of fish sauce
- 1-3 tbsp of pepper powder (White)
- Lime quarter
- 2-4 cloves of garlic
- 1 minced shallot
- 1/3 c. of finely cut sausage of your preference
- 1 handful of fresh spinach
- 1 Fresh green onion that is cut into pieces
- A handful of cilantro

Instructions

1. Place a small quantity of cooking oil of your choice into your Ninja Foodi pan.
2. Get your Ninja Foodi to heat up by pressing the setting function Sear/Sauté
3. Crack the eggs into a large-sized bowl.
4. Add the fish sauce and the pepper
5. Wisk until you see the bubbles starting to be formed inside the mixture of eggs
6. Add the remaining ingredients and keep whisking again until your mixture is combined
7. Pour your obtained mixture inside your Ninja foodi pan
8. Cook for about 2 to 3 minutes
9. Once ready; serve and enjoy your omelette with a little bit of cilantro!

Nutrition Information

Calories: 296, Fat: 17g, Carbohydrates: 24g, Dietary Fiber: 0g, Protein: 10g

Recipe 17: Breakfast Quiche

TIME TO PREPARE
10 minutes

COOK TIME
30 Minutes

SERVING
5 People

Ingredients

- 8 Large eggs
- ¼ cup of heavy cream
- 2 teaspoons of kosher salt
- 2 Tablespoons of Butter, for greasing
- 1 Refrigerated pie
- 5 Slices of uncooked bacon, chopped into strips of about ¼ inch each
- 1 Small, peeled and diced onion
- 1 Bag of about 6 ounces of fresh spinach
- 1 Bunch of finely chopped fresh chives
- ¼ Pound of grated Swiss cheese

Instructions

1. In a large bowl, combine the eggs with the cream and the salt until you get a smooth mixture
2. Grease your Ninja multi-purpose pan with butter.
3. Place the pie crust in the pan and cover the bottom of the pan making sure to push into sides; then set the pan aside
4. Select the SEAR/SAUTÉ and set it to HIGH; then preheat for about 3 minutes
5. After about 3 minutes, add the bacon to the pot and cook while stirring for about 3 minutes; then add in the onion and cook for about 3 minutes
6. Add the spinach and cook for about 2 minutes
7. Remove the pot from the Foodi and place it on surface that is heat resistant
8. Stir in the egg mixture with the cheese and the chives
9. Transfer the mixture to a bowl and set it aside
10. Place the pot back into the Foodi and place the pan with the pie dough on a reversible rack; make sure the rack in a low orientation
11. Put the rack with the pan in the pot

12. Close the crisping lid of your Ninja Foodi and press the button BAKE/ROAST; then set the temperature to 400°F, and set time to about 8 minutes; then select the START/STOP to begin.
13. Pour the egg mixture into the crust and close the crisping lid
14. Select the BAKE/ROAST and set the temperature to about 360°F, and the time to 17 to 18 minutes.
15. When the cooking process is complete; remove the pan from the pot; then let the quiche cool in the refrigerator before removing it from the pan
16. Serve and enjoy your quiche!

Nutrition Information

Calories: 440, Fat: 34 g, Carbohydrates: 16g, Dietary Fiber: 0g, Protein: 15g

Recipe 18: Oatmeal Muffins

TIME TO PREPARE
10 minutes

COOK TIME
10 Minutes

SERVING
7 People

Ingredients

- 4 tbsp of Maida flour
- 1 tbsp of walnuts
- ¼ cup of Oats
- ¼ cup of mashed Banana
- ¼ cup of unsalted butter or ¼ of apple sauce
- ¼ cup of powdered Sugar
- ½ tbsp of baking powder
- 1 tbsp of milk

Instructions

1. Press the button function Sear/Sauté to preheat your Ninja Foodi
2. In a bowl, mix all together, the butter and the sugar then add the banana and the walnuts and mix the ingredients very well.
3. Now, in another medium bowl, mix the refined flour, the oats and the baking powder.
4. Add your dry ingredients above your mixture and cut then fold the mixture for around 2 to 4 times.
5. Add a little bit of milk if your batter looks very thick to you.
6. Grease the muffin mould that you will use and after that top each muffin before or after placing lining them in the mould.
7. Press the button function Bake/Roast of your Ninja Foodi cooker and bake the muffins in the preheated Ninja Foodi Air Fryer.
8. Set the temperature to 300°F and set your timer for 10 minutes.
9. Let cool for about 10 minutes; then when it becomes cool, serve it and enjoy a great breakfast.

Nutrition Information

Calories: 83.4, Fat: 1.6g, Carbohydrates: 15.3g, Dietary Fiber: 2g, Protein: 3.4g

Recipe 19: Bacon Egg Cheese Roll

TIME TO PREPARE
8 minutes

COOK TIME
15 Minutes

SERVING
6 People

Ingredients

- 2 tablespoons of butter
- ½ Cup of chopped onion
- ½ Cup of chopped green bell pepper
- 4 large eggs
- 1 Pinch of salt and 1 pinch of pepper
- 6 Slices of sugar-free bacon
- 2/3 cup of shredded cheddar cheese
- 1/3 cup of hot salsa

Instructions

1. Start by melting the butter in a medium non-stick skillet over a medium heat.
2. Add the onion and the peppers and cook for about 3 minutes
3. Whisk the eggs and season with 1 pinch of salt and 1 pinch of pepper.
4. Remove the pan from the heat while your eggs are undercooked
5. Arrange 3 slices of bacon side by side; then place half the quantity of the scrambled egg mixture towards the end
6. Put half the quantity of the cheddar over the eggs; then roll the bacon around the eggs and secure with a toothpick
7. Place in the Ninja steam basket; then close with the lid and press the function button "Air Crisp"
8. Set the temperature to about 350° F for about 15 minutes.
9. Flip over half-way through.
10. Remove from the Ninja Foodi Air fryer; then serve with the salsa for the dipping and enjoy!

Nutrition Information

Calories: 680, Fat: 61 g, Carbohydrates: 9.1g, Dietary Fiber: 2g, Protein: 33g

Recipe 20: Quinoa Breakfast Bowl

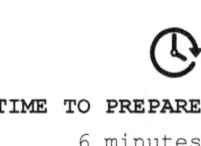

TIME TO PREPARE
6 minutes

COOK TIME
18 Minutes

SERVING
2-3 People

Ingredients

- 1 Cup of quinoa
- 1 ¼ cups of coconut milk
- ¼ to ½ cup of ground cinnamon
- ½ Cup of maple syrup
- 1 Heap cup of water
- ¼ cup of vanilla extract
- ¼ Teaspoon of salt

Instructions

1. Place the quinoa in your Ninja Foodi Pressure cooker; then pour in the coconut milk
2. Pour in the water; the ground cinnamon, the maple syrup, the vanilla extract and the salt
3. Stir your ingredients all together very well before dropping the lid and cook on a high pressure for about 18 minutes
4. Naturally release the pressure and allow the ingredients to cook for about 10 minutes before hitting the button "keep warm/cancel" function button
5. Remove the lid of the Ninja Foodi; then scoop the quinoa into a container
6. Serve and enjoy!

Nutrition Information

Calories: 194, Fat: 1 g, Carbohydrates: 7g, Dietary Fiber: 18g, Protein: 10g

Recipe 21: Ninja Foodi Banana Porridge

TIME TO PREPARE
8 minutes

COOK TIME
10 Minutes

SERVING
3-4 People

Ingredients

- 1 ½ Cups of buckwheat groats
- 1 Cup of chopped bananas
- ½ Cup of raisins
- 3 Cups of milk, rice milk recommended
- ¼ cup of ground cinnamon
- ¼ Cup of vanilla
- ½ Cup of chopped nuts

Instructions

1. Add the buckwheat groats to your Ninja Foddi Pot.
2. Add the rice milk, the raisins, the chopped bananas, the ground cinnamon, and the ¼ vanilla.
3. Close the Ninja pressure lid and turn the valve to sealed position; then set the pressure to High for about 10 minutes
4. After the 10 minutes end; remove the lid of the Ninja Pot; then pour in the chopped nuts
5. Stir your ingredients very well
6. Top with chopped nuts; then serve and enjoy your Banana porridge!

Nutrition Information

Calories: 577, Fat: 14.4g, Carbohydrates: 43.1g, Dietary Fiber: 1 g, Protein: 15g

Recipe 22: Scrambled Eggs

TIME TO PREPARE
15 minutes

COOK TIME
8 Minutes

SERVING
2-3 People

Ingredients

- 2 large eggs
- 10g of unsalted butter
- A pinch of pepper and a pinch of salt

Instructions

1. Crack the eggs in a large bowl and whisk very well
2. Make sure to preheat your Ninja Foodi Air fryer at about 200° F for 4 min.
3. Put a little bit of butter in your preheated Ninja Foodi Air Fryer and wait until it melts.
4. When it is completely melted, place it the pan you'd like to bake it in and slide it in the basket of the Ninja air fryer then spread butter.
5. Lower the heat and bake your eggs for about 6 minutes.
6. When the eggs start to be cooked; add in the cheese, and the tomatoes according to taste
7. Open the Ninja air fryer every two minutes to continue whisking until the entire mixture becomes fluffy and of a golden color, but don't scramble too much.
8. Once your breakfast is ready, take it out of the Ninja air fryer and enjoy eating it with toasted bread.

Nutrition Information

Calories: 78, Fat: 5 g, Carbohydrates: 37g, Dietary Fiber: 3g, Protein: 17g

Recipe 24: Ninja Fried Ravioli

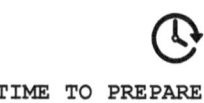

TIME TO PREPARE
7 minutes

COOK TIME
11 Minutes

SERVING
5 People

Ingredients

- 9 oz of refrigerated ravioli - cheese filled
- 2 Large eggs
- 1 Cup of Italian style bread crumbs
- Optional: tomato/ marinara sauce for dipping

Instructions

1. Add the eggs into a shallow dish or bowl; then beat with a fork or whisk very well until you get a smooth mixture
2. In another dish or bowl; place the Italian style bread crumbs
3. Dip the ravioli one at a time into the mixture of the egg; then coat over all the sides
4. Move the ravioli to the bread crumbs; then coat all over very well
5. Shake off any excess of bread crumbs
6. Add in the coated raviolis to the Ninja Foodi air crisp basket in one single layer
7. Set your Ninja Foodi function to Air Crisp and the temperature to about 390° degrees.
8. Air Crisp for about 5 to 6 minutes
9. Repeat until all the raviolis are perfectly toasted.
10. Serve immediately and enjoy your

Nutrition Information

Calories: 206| Fat: 7g | Carbohydrates: 24g | Fiber: 2 g |Protein: 10g

Recipe 25: Egg plant Fries

TIME TO PREPARE
5 minutes

COOK TIME
12 Minutes

SERVING
3 People

Ingredients

- 2 Medium sized Eggplants
- ¼ cup of Cornstarch
- ¼ cup of Olive Oil
- ¼ cup of Water
- 1 pinch of Salt

Instructions

1. Preheat your Ninja Foodi Air fryer to a temperature of 390°F.
2. Cut the eggplants to slices of 10 mm in each.
3. In a big bowl, mix all together the cornstarch,
4. Add the olive oil, the water, and the eggplants
5. Slowly, coat the eggplants
6. Put half the quantity of the eggplant fries in the Foodi Ninja Air crisp basket
7. Cook the components for around 12 minutes or until you see eggplant slices start to get brown.
8. Repeat this process until you see all the eggplant fries are perfectly cooked.
9. Serve and enjoy your appetizer!

Nutrition Information

Calories: 88| Fat: 3.4g | Carbohydrates: 12g | Fiber: 1.4 g |Protein: 2.9g

Recipe 26: Garlic Fried Potatoes

TIME TO PREPARE
6 minutes

COOK TIME
18 Minutes

SERVING
2-3 People

Ingredients

- 4 Sliced Idaho Potatoes
- 4 Tablespoons of melted Butter
- 2 Tablespoons of chopped Garlic
- 2 Tablespoons of Fresh or of dried Parsley
- 3 Tablespoons of grated Parmesan Cheese
- ½ Cup of Water

Instructions

1. Pour the water into the Ninja Foodi pot.
2. Place the cut potatoes in the Air crisp basket and place into the Ninja Foodi pot.
3. Place the pressure lid on top and secure the lid
4. Move the pressure cooker release valve to sealed position; then select the pressure and set it to Low
5. Set the timer to about 3 minutes
6. Press the button function start; then combine the melted butter, the chopped parsley and the parmesan
7. When the pressure cooking time is done; remove the pressure lid; then pour in the melted butter over the fries
8. Close the crisping lid; then press the function Air Crisp
9. Set the temperature to about 400°F and set the timer to 18 minutes
10. Press the button start and check the potatoes after about 10 minutes; you can give a quick shake; ake sure to use the holders as the crisp basket will be hot

11. Serve and enjoy your appetizer!

Nutrition Information

Calories: 180| Fat: 8.6g | Carbohydrates: 23g | Fiber: 2.2 g |Protein: 2.7g

Recipe 27: Zucchini Fries

TIME TO PREPARE
5 minutes

COOK TIME
10 Minutes

SERVING
5 People

Ingredients

- 4 large Zucchini
- ¼ cup of Cornstarch
- ¼ cup of Olive Oil
- ¼ cup of water
- 1 pinch of Salt

Instructions

1. Preheat your Ninja Foodi Air fryer up to 390°F
2. Cut the zucchini to 11 mm X 3 in.
3. In a large bowl; combine the cornstarch with the olive oil
4. Add in the water; then add the zucchini.
5. Mix your ingredients very well and coat the zucchini.
6. Line half of the zucchini fries in your Air Crisp Ninja fryer basket
7. Close the lid of the Ninja Foodi and set the timer to 10 minutes; then press the button "Air Crisp"
8. Air fry the zucchini for about 10 minutes
9. Repeat the same process until you finish frying all the zucchini fries.
10. Remove the lid; then serve and enjoy your fries!

Nutrition Information

Calories: 410| Fat: 23g | Carbohydrates: 33g | Fiber: 2.5 g |Protein: 19g

Recipe 28: Ninja Fried Onion Rings

TIME TO PREPARE
5 minutes

COOK TIME
10 Minutes

SERVING
2-3 People

Ingredients

- 1 medium sized onion (cut it into slices, each of ¼ inch)
- 1 and ¼ cups of flour
- 1 tbsp of baking powder
- 1 tbsp of salt
- 1 large egg
- 1 cup of milk
- ¾ cup of dry bread crumbs or you can use Panko crumbs

Instructions

1. Preheat your Ninja Foodi Air Fryer for about 10 minutes.
2. Separate your onion into slices and then make them look like rings.
3. Stir the mixture all together
4. Add the flour, the baking powder and the salt in a bowl.
5. Dip your onion slices in the mixture of the flour until they become evenly coated.
6. Set the onion rings aside.
7. Whisk your eggs and the milk in the flour with a fork.
8. Dip your floured onion rings into the ready batter to coat it.
9. Spread the bread crumbs above a plate and dredge all the rings in the crumbs
10. Put the onion rings in the Air Crisp Fryer basket and Close the lid
11. Press the button "Air Crisp" for about 10 minutes at a temperature of 390°F
12. Serve your rings, and enjoy it!

Nutrition Information

Calories: 155| Fat: 8g | Carbohydrates: 20g | Fiber: 4 g |Protein: 3g

Recipe 29: Ninja Foodi Vegetable Appetizer

TIME TO PREPARE
10 minutes

COOK TIME
5 Minutes

SERVING
4 People

Ingredients

- 1 Pound of Tomato
- 1 Pound of green pepper
- 1 medium onion
- 3 cloves of garlic
- ½ tbsp of salt
- 1 tbsp of Coriander powder
- 1 tbsp of lemon juice
- 1tbsp of olive oil
- 50 g of black olive
- 3 small eggs

Instructions

1. Preheat your Ninja Foodi Air fryer to about 390°F
2. Line the pepper, the tomato and the onion in the Air Crisp basket of your Foodi Air Fryer
3. Slide the basket in the Ninja Foodi
4. Lock the lid and set your time to 5 minutes by pressing the button "Air Crisp"
5. Open up the lid of the Ninja Foodi; then flip the vegetables to the other side
6. Lock the lid of the Ninja Foodi again
7. After about 5 minutes, remove the vegetables from the Ninja Foodi
8. Peel the skin of the vegetables
9. Place the vegetables in a blender or a mortar with the salt, the coriander powder and process it
10. Once ready, place the mixture on plates and top them with the cooked eggs and the olive with a little bit of oil
11. Enjoy your appetizer!

Nutrition Information:

Calories: 122| Fat: 6.9g | Carbohydrates: 8.78g | Fiber: 1.7 g |Protein: 7.38g

Recipe 30: Ninja Foodi Corn Dogs

TIME TO PREPARE
8 minutes

COOK TIME
15 Minutes

SERVING
7-8 People

Ingredients

- 1 cup of yellow cornmeal
- 1 cup of all-purpose flour
- ¼ cup of white sugar
- 4 teaspoons of baking powder
- ¼ teaspoon of salt
- 1/8 teaspoon of ground black pepper
- 1 cup of milk
- 1 egg
- 16 hot dogs
- ½ cup of vegetable oil

Instructions

1. Preheat your Ninja Foodi to about 350°F for about 5 minutes
2. Combine all together the cornmeal, the flour, the white sugar and the baking powder
3. Add the salt and the pepper
4. In a large bowl; pour in the milk and the egg until the batter becomes smooth.
5. Place the obtained batter in the refrigerator for 5 minutes
6. Bring a pot and boil a quantity of water in it
7. Cook the hot dogs for 7 minutes.
8. Dry the hot dogs with clean paper towels.
9. Line the hot dogs in the Air Crisp Fryer basket of the Ninja Foodi that you have preheated to 350° F
10. Slide the Air Crisp basket in the Ninja Foodi Pot and close the lid
11. Set the timer for about 6 minutes
12. Now, pour the batter in a small bowl.
13. Dip the hot dogs in that batter that you coat all of them
14. Fry the hot dogs in the air fryer until they become lightly browned, about for about 3 minutes.
15. Drain them on paper.
16. Serve and enjoy your appetizer!

Nutrition Information

Calories: 230| Fat: 7.8g | Carbohydrates: 26g | Fiber: 1 g |Protein: 6g

Recipe 31: Fried Kale

TIME TO PREPARE
5 minutes

COOK TIME
8 Minutes

SERVING
3 People

Ingredients

- 2 tbsp of olive oil
- 4 cups of stemmed and packed kale
- 2 teaspoons of vegan seasoning
- 1 tbsp of yeast flakes
- ¼ teaspoon of salt

Instructions

1. Place the oil, the pieces of kale and the ranch seasoning in a large bowl
2. Add the yeast and mix all together in a bowl
3. Dump your coated kale in the Air Crisp Fryer basket of the Ninja Foodi
4. Set the temperature to 390° F
5. Close the lid of your Ninja Foodi with the lid
6. Press the setting button "Air Crisp" and set the timer to 5 minutes (But make sure not to preheat)
7. Shake after 3 minutes.
8. Remove from the Ninja Foodi
9. Serve and enjoy it immediately

Nutrition Information

Calories: 203| Fat: 8g | Carbohydrates: 27g | Fiber: 3 g |Protein: 7g

Recipe 32: Ninja Foodi Falafel

TIME TO PREPARE
5 minutes

COOK TIME
15 Minutes

SERVING
8 People

Ingredients

- 1 bowl of dry or soaked Chick peas
- 2 medium onions
- 4 cloves of garlic
- Leaves of coriander
- A pinch of salt
- 1 teaspoon of baking powder
- Garam Masala

Instructions

1. If you haven't already soaked the peas, soak 1 bowl of chick peas for around 14 hours
2. In a blender, add all your ingredients to get a granular paste.
3. Make small flat balls or tikis by taking a small quantity of the mixture within your palms.
4. Line the patties in the Air Crisp basket of the Ninja Foodi and slide it in you're the Ninja Foodi Air Fryer.
5. Close the lid of the Ninja Foodi and press the button "Air Crisp" and set the timer to about 15 minutes and set the temperature of about 390° F
6. When the time is up, remove the lid when it is safe to do
7. Serve and enjoy your Ninja Air fried Falafel!

Nutrition Information

Calories: 100| Fat: 6g | Carbohydrates: 9g | Fiber: 3 g |Protein: 3g

Recipe 33: Crispy Wontons

TIME TO PREPARE
10 minutes

COOK TIME
7 Minutes

SERVING
8 People

Ingredients

- ¾ lbs of pork (Ground)
- 7 canned water chestnuts
- ¼ cup of shopped onions
- 1 tbsp of Soy Sauce
- 1 Teaspoon of cornstarch
- ½ Teaspoon of salt
- ½ Teaspoon of grated ginger
- 1 package of wonton skins
- 3 spoons of oil
- Ketchup (Tomato ketchup)
- Mustard
- Soy sauce

Instructions

1. Mix the pork with the water chestnuts, the onions, the soy sauce, the cornstarch, the salt and the ginger in a large bowl
2. Add to the mixture ½ tbsp of pork in the middle of every wonton skin.
3. Form a triangle by folding the wonton skin over the fillings.
4. Seal the edges by using the water.
5. Line the triangles in the Air Crisp Fryer basket and slide it into the Ninja Foodi
6. Close the lid of the Ninja Foodi and press the button "Air Crisp"; then set the temperature to 375° F for 7 minutes.
7. Drain the triangles on the paper towels.
8. Serve hot with the mustard, the ketchup or the sour sauce.
9. Enjoy your crispy wontons!

Nutrition Information

Calories: 214.8| Fat: 2.5g | Carbohydrates: 4.7g | Fiber: 0.9g |Protein: 13.9g

Recipe 34: Mini Cheese and salami Pizzas

TIME TO PREPARE
5 minutes

COOK TIME
5 Minutes

SERVING
7 People

Ingredients

- 11 Oz of grated mozzarella
- 13 tsp of marinara sauce made of passata+ 1 garlic clove+ Italian herbs+ 1 pinch of salt and 1 pinch of ground black pepper
- A few dices of salami
- 1 Handful of basil leaves

Instructions

1. Preheat your Ninja Foodi Air Fryer to a temperature of about 390° F
2. Prepare your marinara sauce by mixing the passata can with the garlic with the salt, the pepper and the Italian herbs
3. Garnish with the oregano or the basil
4. Spray your Ninja Foodi Air Fryer pan with cooking spray
5. Place small and round handfuls of mozzarella into your Ninja Air Crisp Fryer Basket but make sure to leave a space around each of the mozzarella rounds
6. Slide the Air Crisp basket in your Ninja Foodi and lock the lid

7. Press the button "Air Crisp" and set the timer to about 4 to 5 minutes
8. Sauté the salami in a pan over a medium heat
9. Once the timer beeps; turn off your Ninja Foodi then set the mozzarella aside to cool
10. Add 1 teaspoon of marinara sauce over each of the pizzas and decorate it with the salami and the ham pieces.
11. Garnish with the chopped basil leaves
12. Serve and enjoy your mini pizzas!

Nutrition Information

Calories: 420| Fat: 21g | Carbohydrates: 41g | Fiber: 0.0g |Protein: 17g

Recipe 35: Cheese Chips

TIME TO PREPARE
5 minutes

COOK TIME
5 Minutes

SERVING
3 People

Ingredients

- 4 Oz of sliced cheddar cheese
- ½ tsp of paprika powder

Instructions

1. Preheat your Ninja Foodi Air Fryer to a temperature of about 390° F
2. Line the Air Ninja Air Crisp Basket with a baking sheet
3. Place the slices of cheese in the Air Crisp Basket pan
4. Sprinkle the paprika powder over the cheese; then Air Crisp Basket in the Ninja Foodi and lock the lid
5. Press the button "Air Crisp" and set the timer to about 10 minutes and set the temperature to 360°F
6. When the timer beeps; turn off your Ninja Foodi Air Fryer and set aside to cool for 5 minutes
7. Serve and enjoy with your favorite guacamole!

Nutrition Information

Calories: 290| Fat: 19g | Carbohydrates: 24g | Fiber: 0g |Protein: 6g

Recipe 36: Ninja Foodi Pretzels

TIME TO PREPARE
8 minutes

COOK TIME
6 Minutes

SERVING
8 People

Ingredients

- 8oz of Gluten-Free Pretzels or Regular Pretzels (Mini or Stick Pretzels)
- 1 Packet of Dry Ranch Seasoning
- ¼ Teaspoon of Garlic Powder
- 1 Tablespoon of Olive Oil Spray

Instructions

1. Line the Ninja Foodi Air Fryer with an aluminum foil and spray the Air Crisp fryer basket.
2. Put the pretzels in Air Crisp basket and top with the ranch seasoning and the garlic powder.
3. Spray a little quantity of olive oil spray and combine the pretzels very well.
4. Cook in the Ninja Air crisp air fryer at 350°F for 3 minutes.
5. Remove the pretzels; and open the lid; then spray with the olive oil spray and mix up very well
6. Cook again for about 3 additional minutes.
7. Remove the pretzels or just open the lid; then spray with olive oil spray and mix up once more.
8. Finish the cooking process for about 2 additional minutes or until the pretzels become crispy.
9. Serve and enjoy your snack!

Nutrition Information

Calories: 98| Fat: 2g | Carbohydrates: 5418g | Fiber: 1g |Protein: 3g

Recipe 37: French Sticks

TIME TO PREPARE
10 minutes

COOK TIME
10 Minutes

SERVING
10 People

Ingredients

- 5 pieces of sliced bread, you are free to choose the thickness of the bread slices.
- 2 tbsp of warm butter to use for buttering your bread.
- 2 Large beaten eggs gently
- A pinch of salt
- A pinch of cinnamon
- Ground cloves
- Nutmeg
- Icing sugar to use for garnish

Instructions

1. Preheat your Ninja Foodi Air fryer up to 350° F.
2. In a large bowl, beat all together the eggs, a pinch of salt, cinnamon, nutmeg and ground cloves, cinnamon, and small pinches of both nutmeg and ground cloves.
3. Make sure to butter each side of the bread slices you prepared and sliced into strips
4. Dip each strip of bread in the mixture of the eggs and arrange them in the Air Crisp basket, maybe you will find yourself cooking in two batches.
5. After exactly 2 minutes, pause your Ninja Foodi Air fryer, take your pan out and make sure that you put the pan on a safe surface, then spray the your bread with your cooking spray on the second side as well.
6. Now return the pan to your fryer and cook your breakfast for additional more minutes, a couple of minutes will be enough.
7. When the egg and the bread acquire a golden colour, remove it from the Ninja Foodi Air fryer and serve it immediately.
8. You can use whipped cream for garnish and you can add maple syrup too.

1. Enjoy!

Nutrition Information

Calories: 370.6| Fat: 19.3g | Carbohydrates: 44.9g | Fiber: 1.5g |Protein: 6.5g

Recipe 38: Sausage balls

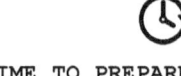
TIME TO PREPARE
10 minutes

COOK TIME
6 Minutes

SERVING
12 People

Ingredients

- 1 lb of Hot Breakfast Sausage
- 2 cups of shredded Sharp Cheddar Cheese
- 4 Cups of Bisquick

Instructions

1. Place the sausage in a mixer and process at a low speed
2. Add in about 2 cups of cheese and continue mixing at a low speed
3. Add in one cup of Bisquick at a time; then mix at a low speed until all the four cups are used
4. Roll the mixture into balls of about 1 to 1 1/2 " of diameter balls
5. Store in an airtight container in the refrigerator
6. Place one dozen of balls into your Ninja Foodi Air Fryer and press the button "Air Crisp" at a temperature of about 390°F for about 5 to 6 minutes shaking through the cooking process
7. Serve and enjoy!

Nutrition Information

Calories: 180| Fat: 15g | Carbohydrates: 2g | Fiber: 0g |Protein: 9g

Recipe 39: Chicken Bites

TIME TO PREPARE
10 minutes

COOK TIME
15 Minutes

SERVING
10 People

Ingredients

- 1 Pound of shredded; ground chicken
- ½ Cup of yellow onion, diced
- ¼ Cup of diced red bell pepper
- 2 Tablespoons of minced fresh mint
- 2 Tablespoons of red curry paste
- 1 Teaspoon of ground cumin
- 1 and ½ teaspoon of minced fresh ginger
- ½ Teaspoon of ground coriander
- ½ Teaspoon of sea salt
- ¼ Teaspoon of black pepper

Instructions

1. Preheat your Ninja Foodi Air fryer to about 390°F
2. Mix all of your ingredients into a bowl and shape it into about 15 meatballs and place it in the Air Crisp basket
3. Close the lid of the Ninja Foodi air fryer and set the timer to about 15 minutes and the temperature to about 350°F
4. When the timer beeps, remove the meat balls from the Ninja Foodi Air Fryer; then serve and enjoy a mouthwatering appetizer!

Nutrition Information

Calories: 294| Fat: 16g | Carbohydrates: 15g | Fiber: 0.8g |Protein: 12g

Recipe 40: Stuffed Potatoes

TIME TO PREPARE
12 minutes

COOK TIME
15 Minutes

SERVING
5 People

Ingredients

- 5 large potatoes
- 8 Slices of bread
- 2 Seeded and diced potatoes
- 1 Bunch of chopped coriander
- 2 chopped onions
- ½ Teaspoon of turmeric
- ½ Teaspoon of mustard seeds
- 2 Sprigs of curry leaf
- 2 Tablespoons of olive oil
- 1 Pinch of salt

Instructions

1. Preheat your Ninja Foodi to about 350° F
2. Boil the potatoes into salted water
3. Peel; then mash the boiled potatoes
4. In a saucepan, heat about 1 teaspoon of olive oil and after that add the mustard seeds.
5. Add the onions and sauté the ingredients for about 1 minute
6. Add the potatoes and the salt; then mix very well.
7. Add the curry leaves and sauté for 30 seconds.
8. Add the potatoes and adjust the taste of salt and the pepper
9. Shape the mixture into about 8 portions of even size; then keep it aside
10. Trim the sides of the bread; then wet it with a little bit of water
11. Press down the bread with your hand and Trim the bread from the sides and wet it completely with water, press the bread with your palm and gently put your potato of an oval shape and roll your bread in the shape of spindle
12. Seal the potato edges and brush all the breads with

     a little drizzle of oil.

13. Arrange the stuffed potatoes in the Air Crisp basket; then close the lid

14. Press the button "Air Crisp" and set the timer to about 15 minutes and the temperature to 365° F

15. When the timer beeps, serve and enjoy your delicious stuffed potatoes!

Nutrition Information

Calories: 164.4| Fat: 0.8g | Carbohydrates: 32.8g | Fiber: 3.3g |Protein: 7.5g

Recipe 41: Cauliflower bites

TIME TO PREPARE
15 minutes

COOK TIME
20 Minutes

SERVING
8-9 People

Ingredients

- 1 Pound of organic cauliflower
- ½ Pound of chicken liver
- 1 Teaspoon of unrefined sea salt
- 2 Tablespoons of organic butter
- 3 Eggs
- 1/3 Cup of flour

Instructions

1. Start by cooking the cauliflower until it becomes tender
2. Drain the cauliflower and set it aside
3. Preheat your Ninja Foodi to about 350 °F
4. Add the coconut oil; the chicken liver and a little bit of salt to the purée of the cauliflower and crack in the eggs; then whisk very well until your ingredients are completely combined
5. Sift in the coconut flour and mix very well; set the mixture aside for about 10 minutes
6. Let the mass stand for 10 minutes.
7. Prepare a baking sheet and line it with a baking paper
8. Prepare a small pastry bag that has quite a large star tip
9. Start piping the cauliflower rosette over the parchment paper
10. Arrange your duchess cauliflowers on a greased baking sheet in the Air Crisp basket of your Ninja

Foodi and close the lid
11. Press the button "Air Crisp" and set the timer to about 20 minutes
12. When the timer beeps, remove the cauliflower duchess
13. Serve and enjoy your delicious cauliflower bites!

Nutrition Information

Calories: 215.7| Fat: 10.2g | Carbohydrates: 15.5g | Fiber: 1.1g |Protein: 14.7g

Recipe 42: Samosa

TIME TO PREPARE
5 minutes

COOK TIME
6 Minutes

SERVING
3 People

Ingredients

- Teaspoon of ketchup
- 2 Cups of cubed potato
- 2 Teaspoons of extra-virgin olive oil
- ½ Teaspoon of ground turmeric
- ¼ Teaspoon of kosher salt
- 1/8 Teaspoon of ground red pepper
- ¼ Cup of fresh chopped parsley
- 1/3 Cup of thinly sliced green onions
- 4 Sheets of frozen thawed phyllo dough
- 2 Tablespoons of cooking spray
- 3 to 4 chilled eggs
- ½ cup of crumbled feta cheese
- ¼ Teaspoon of black

Instructions

1. Start by putting the potatoes into a medium saucepan and cover it with water; let the potatoes simmer on a low heat for about 10 to 15 minute
2. Preheat your Ninja Food Air Fryer to about 390° F by pressing the button "Sear/Sauté"
3. Heat the oil in a shallow wok and combine in it the potatoes, the turmeric, the salt, and the ground red pepper; then sauté for about 6 minutes or until the edges become crispy.
4. Add the parsley and the green onions; then cook for about minutes,
5. Remove from the heat and put 1 sheet of the phyllo dough above a large cutting board
6. Coat the phyllo with the cooking spray and fold the sheet into half
7. Coat the bottom third of your phyllo with a little bit of cooking spray
8. Fold the bottom third up and put ¼ of the cooked potatoes into the form a circle into the center
9. Crack in 1 egg into the center of the potatoes and sprinkle the ¼ of the feta over the egg.
10. Sprinkle with a little bit of black pepper and
11. Whisk the egg white with 1 teaspoon of water into a bowl and stir very well

- pepper
- 1 Egg white
- 1 teaspoon water
- ¼ Cup of chopped fresh cilantro

12. Brush your phyllo packets with the egg white mixture and arrange it in the Air Crisp Basket of the Ninja Foodi Air fryer
13. Close the lid and press the button "Air Crisp" and set the timer for about 9 to 10 minutes and the temperature to about 390° F
14. When the timer beeps, serve and enjoy your crunchy samosas hot!

Nutrition Information

Calories: 308| Fat: 12g | Carbohydrates: 32g | Fiber: 1g |Protein: 4g

Recipe 43: Ninja Foodi Chicken Enchiladas

TIME TO PREPARE
6 minutes

COOK TIME
6-7 Minutes

SERVING
2-3 People

Ingredients

- 1 Red sauce of Enchilada Sauce; it should be low carb sauce
- 9 Low Carb Tortillas
- 16 Oz of cheddar cheese
- 16 Oz of chicken cuts or shredded chicken
- 1 Small sliced green onion
- Finely chopped cilantro for garnishing

Instructions

1. Put the sauce on the stove to heat up; meanwhile, let the shred the chicken meat and season it with pepper and salt.
2. If the sauce tastes good and became thick, remove it from the heat
3. Grate your cheese and set it aside.
4. Preheat your air fryer to about 390°Fahrenheit
5. Pour a little quantity of sauce into the Air Crisp Basket of your Ninja Foodie Air Fryer
6. Place a tortilla above a hard working surface and put around 2 tablespoons of the shredded cheese into the middle of the enchiladas
7. Add about ¼ cup of chicken right on your cheese
8. Roll up your tortilla and put it with the side down into a baking tray that fits your air fryer basket
9. Repeat the same process with the remaining ingredients until you finally finish all of it
10. Pour the sauce above your enchiladas and add the remaining quantity of the cheese right on top of it.
11. Sprinkle the onions on your enchiladas and put it in

       the Air Crisp basket of the Ninja Foodi
12. Close the lid of the Ninja Foodi and set the timer to about 30 minutes at a temperature of 360° F by pressing the button "Air Crisp"
13. When the timer beeps, remove the enchiladas from the air fryer and serve it; enjoy!

Nutrition Information

Calories: 425| Fat: 21g | Carbohydrates: 52g | Fiber: 0g |Protein: 6g

Recipe 44: Stuffed Peppers

TIME TO PREPARE
10 minutes

COOK TIME
20 Minutes

SERVING
13 People

Ingredients

For your stuffed jalapeños:
- 13 Medium or large jalapenos
- 1 Cup of sharp shredded cheddar cheese
- 8 Oz of softened cream cheese
- 2 Cups of shredded and diced cooked chicken
- ⅓ Cup of salsa Verde
- ½ Teaspoon of garlic powder
- ½ Teaspoon of kosher salt
- 1 Teaspoon of Cajun seasoning

To prepare the breading:
- 1 Cup of pulverized pork rinds
- ½ Teaspoon of Cajun seasoning

Instructions

To prepare your stuffed Jalapeños:
1. Cut the tops of the peppers and scoop out its insides
2. Put the peppers above a tray and microwave it for about 2 minutes until it becomes soft.
3. Combine the cheddar cheese, the cream cheese, the chicken or the turkey
4. Add the salsa Verde, the garlic powder, the salt and the Cajun seasoning into a deep bowl and combine very well until the mixture becomes creamy
5. Spoon your mixture in the jalapeños.
6. In a small bowl, combine the rinds of pork dust and add the Cajun seasoning.
7. Roll your cream cheese onto the side of your stuffed jalapeños in the Cajun pork rinds until it becomes all coated.
8. Arrange the jalapeños in the Air Crisp basket of the Ninja Air fryer
9. Close the lid of the Ninja Foodi Air fryer and press the button "Air Crisp"
10. Set the timer to about 20 minutes and the temperature to around 390° F

11. When the timer beeps, remove the jalapeños and let it aside to cool for several minutes
12. Serve and enjoy!

Nutrition Information

Calories: 242.8| Fat: 9g | Carbohydrates: 22.1g | Fiber: 3g |Protein: 19.9g

CHAPTER 4: VEGETABLE RECIPES

Recipe 45: Vegetable Ratatouille

TIME TO PREPARE
6 minutes

COOK TIME
33 Minutes

SERVING
4-5 People

Ingredients

- 1 Large eggplant
- 1 Medium zucchini
- 1 Yellow squash
- 4 Large tomatoes
- 1 Medium onion
- ½ Tablespoon of olive oil in a spritzer bottle
- 2 Bulbs of roasted Garlic
- 4 Sprigs of Thyme or ½ teaspoon of dried Thyme leaves
- 2 Sprigs of oregano or ½ teaspoon of dried oregano
- ½ teaspoon of dried basil leaves
- 2.25 Oz of black olives sliced with the juice
- 1 Teaspoon of Minor's Vegetable Base
- 1 Pinch of crushed red pepper flakes

Instructions

1. Cut the vegetables into chunks of about 1 ½ inches each
2. Place the vegetables in the Air Crisp basket of the Ninja Foodi
3. Place the basket in the inner pot and season with 1 pinch of salt and 1 pinch of black pepper
4. Spritz with olive oil and toss the vegetables around to coat with the oil and the seasonings.
5. With the TenderCrisp lid, set the function broil function to about 15 minutes.
6. When the time is up, toss your vegetables around; then spritz a few additional times with olive oil; then broil for about 15 more minutes
7. Dump the Air crisp basket with the vegetables in the inner pot; then add in the roasted garlic; 1 teaspoon of Minors vegetable base or of fresh herbs; then add ½ tsp of dried basil leaves, the black olives with the juice and the crushed red pepper flakes.
8. Stir and place the pressure lid on; then set the pressure to LOW for about 3 minute and make sure to turn the valve to sealed position; then start.
9. When the time is done, do a quick release.
10. Serve and enjoy!

Nutrition Information

Calories: 138| Fat: 3 g | Carbohydrates: 27g | Fiber: 7g |Protein: 4g

Recipe 46: Ninja Foodi Cooked Vegetables

TIME TO PREPARE
5 minutes

COOK TIME
10 Minutes

SERVING
3-4 People

Ingredients

- 1 Tablespoon of olive oil
- 1 Pound of thinly sliced chorizo, chicken sausage
- 1 Heaping cup of white rice
- 1 Teaspoon of saffron
- ¼ Teaspoon of fine sea salt
- 1 Cup of chunky and thick salsa
- 1 Cup of chicken stock
- ½ Cup of chopped roasted red pepper
- 1 Cup of frozen peas
- 1 wedged lemon wedges
  Chopped parsley

Instructions

1. Slice the zucchini and the yellow squash into dials.
2. Slice the mushrooms into half; then put all the vegetables in a large bowl and toss your ingredients very well together.
3. Pour the olive oil over the top and gently toss
4. Sprinkle in all the seasonings in a large bowl and toss once additional time
5. Add about half of the vegetables into your Ninja Foodi
6. Close the Ninja Foodi fryer with the lid; then press the button function "Air Crisp" and set the timer to about 10 minutes and the temperature to about 400°F
7. Remove; then serve and enjoy your meal!

Nutrition Information

Calories: 185| Fat: 18g | Carbohydrates: 5g | Fiber: 2g |Protein: 2g

Recipe 47: Ninja Foodi Steamed Broccoli

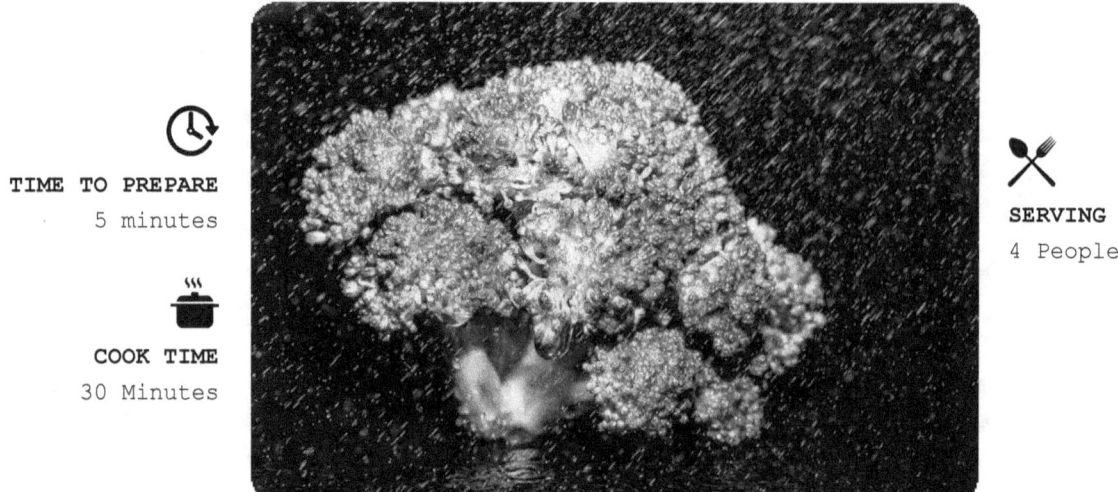

TIME TO PREPARE
5 minutes

COOK TIME
30 Minutes

SERVING
4 People

Ingredients

- 1 to 2 heads of broccoli, cut into florets
- ½ Cup of water
- 6 Minced garlic cloves
- 1 Tablespoon of peanut oil
- 1 Tablespoon of Chinese rice wine
- ⅛ tsp to ¼ tsp of Fine Sea Salt

Instructions

1. Pour ½ cup of cold tap water in your Ninja Foodi Pressure Cooker
2. Place a rack in your Ninja Foodi and place the broccoli florets in the Air Crisp Basket; then slide the Air Crisp Basket in the Ninja Foodi
3. Lock the Ninja Foodi cooker lid and press the button STEAM by pressing the button for about 10 minutes
4. Turn off the Ninja Foodi and do a quick release.
5. Open the lid of the Ninja Foodi, then remove the broccoli and quickly place it in an ice bath
6. Drain the water; then set it aside to air dry it
7. Remove the hot water from your Ninja Foodi; then press the button "SEAR/SAUTé"
8. Sauté the garlic and the Broccoli; then add 1 tablespoon of peanut oil into the Ninja Foodi Pot
9. Make sure to add a little quantity of oil to the bottom
10. Sauté the garlic for about 25 to 30 seconds; then pour in the broccoli and stir for about 30 seconds
11. Season with 1 pinch of salt and 1 pinch of pepper
12. Add in 1 tablespoon of rice wine and stir; then season to taste
13. Serve and enjoy your dish!

Nutrition Information

Calories: 62 | Fat: 12g | Carbohydrates: 0g | Fiber: 4g | Protein: 5g

Recipe 48: Potato with bacon

TIME TO PREPARE
5 minutes

COOK TIME
20 Minutes

SERVING
4 People

Ingredients

- 4 medium potatoes; scrub and cut them into cubes.
- 1 large cut Onion
- 1 Red Pepper
- 2 tbsp of Bacon Grease, or Olive Oil
- 1 and ½ teaspoons of smoked salt or sea salt
- 1 teaspoon of onion Powder
- 1 teaspoon of garlic Powder
- 1 teaspoon of Paprika
- Chopped bacon for garnishing

Instructions

1. Place the potatoes you have already scrubbed in a strainer and put it in a bowl then cover it with water. Let it soak for around 25 minutes.
2. Dice the onions and the red pepper, and while the potatoes are soaking, mix the seasonings
3. Drain the potatoes and dry them very well, then put them in a bowl.
4. Add the onions, the peppers and the bacon grease then mix very well
5. Put the mixture of the potato in the Air Crisp basket; then slide it into your Ninja Foodi and close the lid of
6. Press the button "Air Crisp" and cook at a degree of 380° F for around 20 minutes
7. Shake the Air Crisp basket through the cooking process and if you notice it needs more time, make it longer, your potatoes should be tender.
8. Dump the mixture of potatoes into a large bowl and season it then mix it
9. Serve and enjoy your potatoes with the chopped bacon!

Nutrition Information

Calories: 249.6 | Fat: 3.4g | Carbohydrates: 48.4g | Fiber: 6.1g | Protein: 7.5g

Recipe 49: Ninja Foodi Beets

TIME TO PREPARE
5 minutes

COOK TIME
24 Minutes

SERVING
3-4 People

Ingredients

- 6 Medium beets of about 1 ¾ lbs
- 1 Cup of (250ml) cold water

Instructions

1. Prepare the Beets; then rub and wash the beets under tap water
2. If the beets have greens and stems, trim off; then save for another dish
3. Trim off; then discard the roots
4. Pour 1 cup of water in your Ninja Foodi; then place the Air Crisp Basket in the Ninja Foodi and place the beets in the Basket
5. Close the lid and press the button "PRESSURE" and set the timer for about 24 minutes; make sure the valve is in sealed position
6. Do a quick release pressure method when the time is up and turn the knob to venting position
7. Carefully open the lid; then serve and enjoy the beets!

Nutrition Information

Calories: 58| Fat: 1g | Carbohydrates: 13g | Fiber: 4g |Protein: 12.7g

Recipe 50: Ninja Foodi Pinto Beans

TIME TO PREPARE
7 minutes

COOK TIME
40 Minutes

SERVING
4 People

Ingredients

- 1 Pound of dry pinto beans
- 1 Small, finely chopped onion
- 1 Finely minced garlic clove
- 1 Bunch of tied cilantro stems
- 7 Cups of water
- 1 and ½ teaspoons of kosher salt
- 1 teaspoon of ground cumin

Instructions

1. Start by combining all the ingredients in your Ninja Foodi
2. Cover the Ninja Foodi with a lid and lock; make sure the valve is in sealed position
3. Press the button function "Pressure" and set the time to about 40 minutes
4. Do a natural steam release
5. When it is safe to do, open the lid of the Ninja Foodi
6. Serve and enjoy your Ninja Pinto beans!

Nutrition Information

Calories: 245| Fat: 1g | Carbohydrates: 45g | Fiber: 15g |Protein: 15g

Recipe 51: Vegetables Pie

TIME TO PREPARE
10 minutes

COOK TIME
40 Minutes

SERVING
5 People

Ingredients

- 4 Tablespoons of unsalted butter
- ½ large chopped onion
- 1 and ½ cups of diced carrots
- 1 and ½ cups of diced celery
- 2 Minced garlic cloves
- 3 Cups of diced red potatoes
- 1 Cup of vegetable broth
- ½ Cup of frozen peas
- ½ Cup of frozen corn
- 1 Tablespoon of chopped fresh Italian parsley
- 2 Teaspoons of fresh thyme leaves
- ¼ Cup of flour
- ½ Cup of heavy cream
- 1 Pinch of salt
- 1 Pinch of pepper

Instructions

1. Press the button "SEAR/SAUTE" and set to MD:HI; then press the button "START" and preheat for about 5 minutes
2. Melt the butter in a pot, then add the onions; the carrots and the celery and sauté for about 3 minutes
3. Stir the garlic into the veggies and cook for about 30 seconds while stirring
4. Press the button "STOP"; then add the potatoes and the broth and stir
5. Place the lid on the pot and set the valve to SEAL
6. Select the button PRESSURE and Press START;
7. When the cooking process is done, do a quick release pressure; then remove the lid
8. Add the peas, the corn, the thyme and the parsley to the pot and sprinkle with the flour; then mix very well and add in the heavy cream
9. Select the SEAR/SAUTE and set to a MD:HI; then Press the button START and cook while stirring constantly for about 2 to 3 minutes
10. Press the STOP button; then season the mixture with 1 pinch of salt and 1 pinch of pepper
11. Place the pie crust over the vegetable mixture; then

- 1 prepared pie crust

fold over the edges of the crust to fit the pot.
12. Make a small vent into the center of the crust.
13. Cover then Ninja Foodi with the crisping lid; then select the setting button BROIL and set the time to about 10 minutes
14. Press the button START.
15. After the time is up, transfer the inner pot to a heat proof surface; then let pie sit for about 10 minutes
16. Serve and enjoy your dish!

Nutrition Information

Calories: 194 | Fat: 5g | Carbohydrates: 26.932g | Fiber: 0g | Protein: 4g

Recipe 52: Ninja Foodi Green Beans

TIME TO PREPARE
5 minutes

COOK TIME
2 Minutes

SERVING
3-4 People

Ingredients

- ½ cups of diced onion
- 4 Slices of diced bacon
- 1 Teaspoon of salt
- ½ teaspoon of pepper
- 6 Cups of green beans about 2 lbs with the ends removed
- ¼ Cups of vegetable broth or of water
- 1 Teaspoon of olive oil

Instructions

1. Set your Foodi on the setting sauté mode; then add the olive oil, the bacon and the diced onions.
2. Cook until the bacon is cooked; then turn off the Ninja Foodi
3. Pour in the chicken broth; then deglaze the pot
4. Add the cut fresh green beans into the Ninja Foodi pot with the broth or the water
5. Stir; then season with salt and pepper on top.
6. Close the Ninja Foodi with the pressure cooker lid and steam valve; then cook on High for about 2 minutes
7. When the time is up, turn off your Ninja Foodi and do a quick release
8. Remove; then serve and enjoy your dish!

Nutrition Information

Calories: 106| Fat: 7g | Carbohydrates: 9g | Fiber: 3g |Protein: 4g

Recipe 53: Garlicky Tomatoes

TIME TO PREPARE
5 minutes

COOK TIME
4 Minutes

SERVING
5 People

Ingredients

- 4 large tomatoes
- 1 tbsp of olive oil
- A pinch of salt
- A pinch of fresh black pepper
- 1 minced clove of garlic
- ½ teaspoon of dried thyme
- 3 tbsp of vinegar

Instructions

1. Pre-heat your Ninja Foodi up to 390° F.
2. Cut the tomatoes into halves and remove the seeds
3. Put your cut tomatoes in a big bowl and toss it with the oil, the salt, the pepper, the garlic and the thyme.
4. Put the tomatoes in the Air Crisp basket
5. Place the basket in the Ninja Foodi and lock the lid; then press the button "AIR CRISP"
6. Set the timer to 15 minutes and the heat at 390° F.
7. Make sure the edges shouldn't be cooked until they become brown.
8. Remove the tomatoes and let them cool aside.
9. You can use this side dish with any crostini, meat or even dish.
10. Drizzle a little bit of vinegar.
11. Serve and enjoy!

Nutrition Information

Calories: 40 | Fat: 0g | Carbohydrates: 9g | Fiber: 1g | Protein: 1g

Recipe 54: Couscous with chickpeas

TIME TO PREPARE
5 minutes

COOK TIME
9 Minutes

SERVING
4 People

Ingredients

- 1 and ¾ cups of vegetable broth
- 1 teaspoon of ground coriander
- ½ teaspoon of ground cardamom
- ½ teaspoon of ground turmeric
- ½ teaspoon of hot pepper sauce
- ¼ teaspoon of salt
- 1/8 teaspoon of ground cinnamon
- 1 cup of julienned carrots
- 1 cup or 2 of rinsed and drained chickpeas
- 1 cup of frozen peas

Instructions

1. In your Ninja Foodi Air, pour in the broth, the coriander, the cardamom, the turmeric, the pepper sauce, the salt and the cinnamon.
2. Pour 2 tbsp of oil
3. Set the temperature to 340° F
4. Press the button timer SEAR/SAUTE and set to about 5 minutes
5. Add the carrots and sauté for 5 minutes.
6. After the timer goes off, remove the ingredients from the Ninja Foodi
7. Transfer the ingredients to a sauce pan.
8. Boil the mixture.
9. Add the chickpeas and the frozen peas.
10. Let simmer, but uncovered this time for 4 minutes.
11. Turn off the heat. Stir in the couscous.
12. Now, cover the couscous and let it boil for 5 minutes.
13. Fluff the mixture using a fork.
14. Sprinkle the couscous using mint

- 1 cup of quick-cooking couscous
- 2 tbsp of chopped fresh mint

15. Serve and enjoy your couscous

Nutrition Information

Calories: 164.3| Fat: 1.4g | Carbohydrates: 33.1g | Fiber: 4.9g |Protein: 3.41g

Recipe 55: Egg and Vegetables Salad

TIME TO PREPARE
5 minutes

COOK TIME
7 Minutes

SERVING
3-4 People

Ingredients

- 6 lightly cooked eggs
- 2 peeled and chopped avocados
- 1 and ½ cup of chopped tomatoes
- ½ cup of cut of red onion
- 1 pinch of salt
- 1 pinch of ground black pepper.
- and ground black pepper
- 2 tbsp of mayonnaise
- 2 tbsp of sour cream
- 1 tbsp of lemon juice
- 9 drops of hot sauce

Instructions

1. In the Air Crisp basket of the Ninja Foodi, place the thinly sliced eggs.
2. Add the tomatoes, the red onion, the salt, and the pepper all together in a big bowl.
3. Place the Air Crisp Basket in the Ninja Foodi and close the lid
4. Set the timer to 7 minutes.
5. Set the temperature to 350°F
6. Once the timer beeps; turn off the heat, and place the ingredients in a bowl.
7. Stir in the mayonnaise
8. Add in the sour cream, the lemon juice, and the hot sauce into the mixture of the mixed egg.
9. Make sure the mixture is evenly coated.
10. Garnish with the avocado.
11. Serve your salad and enjoy your dish!

Nutrition Information

Calories: 260| Fat: 23g | Carbohydrates: 1g | Fiber: 0g |Protein: 11g

CHAPTER 5: FISH AND SEAFOOD RECIPES

Recipe 56: Ninja Foodi Fish and Chips

TIME TO PREPARE
5 minutes

COOK TIME
15 Minutes

SERVING
3-4 People

Ingredients	Instructions
<ul><li>3 to 4 Fish Fillets (If you are to choose, the catfish is the best)</li><li>1 Large beaten egg</li><li>3 Slices of Bread to be made into fine breadcrumbs</li><li>1 Bag of Tortilla Chips</li><li>1 Lemon, juiced</li><li>1Tbsp of Parsley</li><li>1 Pinch of Salt</li><li>1 Pinch of Pepper</li></ul>	1. Cut your fish fillets into half in order to make around four pieces of fish that are ready to be cooked. 2. Season your fish using lemon zest 3. Place one half of lemon by the side of the fish 4. In a food processor, grind the lemon rind, the parsley, the tortillas, the salt and the pepper with the bread. 5. Place your fish in a tray and coat it with the beaten egg, then the breadcrumbs. 6. Arrange your fish in the Air Crisp basket of your Ninja Foodi 7. Slide the Air Crisp Basket in the Ninja Foodi and close the lid 8. Press the Button AIR CRISP and set the timer to 15 minutes and the temperature to about 340°F!

Nutrition Information

Calories: 263 | Fat: 15g | Carbohydrates: 28g | Fiber: 4g | Protein: 4g

Recipe 57: Pomfret Fish Fry

TIME TO PREPARE
6 minutes

COOK TIME
15 Minutes

SERVING
3 People

Ingredients

- 3 lb of boneless fish
- 4 Onions
- 3 lb of silver Pomfret
- 1 pinch of ground black pepper
- 1 tbsp of turmeric powder
- 3 pinches of Red Chilli powder
- 1 Tbsp of salt or as required.
- ¾ teaspoons of ginger/Garlic paste
- 3 pinches of Cumin Powder
- 2 Teaspoons of Lemon Juice –
- 4 curry leaves.
- Olive oil or Coconut Oil

Instructions

1. Start by cleaning the fish.
2. Remove the fish wastes from the bellies.
3. Cut the fish finely to form a nice shape.
4. Rub your fish above a hard surface.
5. Above the cutting board and clean the fish with the salt.
6. Wash the fish using clean water and let it fish soak into the lemon juice in order to clean the fish from any unpleasant smell.
7. After 30 minutes, take your fish out of lemon juice and wash it with clean water.
8. Draw diagonal shaped slits on the fish.
9. Now as for preparing your Masala, combine the black pepper with the salt, the garlic paste, the lemon juice and the turmeric powder.
10. Rub the mixture above the fish and in its inside. Then stuff your curry leaves on your fish and leave it n the fridge for 30 minutes to absorb the seasoning.
11. Take out fish and remove the leaves of the curry.
12. Arrange the fish in the Air Crisp basket of the Ninja Foodi; then pour in 2 tbsp of oil it

13. Close the lid of the Ninja Foodi and press the button Air Crisp; then bake it for about 15 minutes.
14. Set the temperature to about 340° F
15. Serve and enjoy your fish!

Nutrition Information

Calories: 230| Fat: 15g | Carbohydrates: 0g | Fiber: 0g |Protein: 24g

Recipe 58: Tandoori Fish

TIME TO PREPARE
8 minutes

COOK TIME
15 Minutes

SERVING
3 People

Ingredients

- 1 Whole fish 1 (about 2lb)
- 1 tbsp of Garam Masala
- 3tbsp of cooking oil
- 1 teaspoon of dry ground
- 8 Cloves of Garlic
- 2 Cubes of green Papaya
- 1teaspoon of turmeric powder
- ½ teaspoon of cumin seeds
- 1tbqp of red chillies powder
- 2 lemons' juice.
- Salt and black pepper.

Instructions

1. Cut and scale the fish, then wash it very well.
2. Wipe your fish dry and apply your ground paste over the inside and out of the fishes
3. Make four slits or gashes on both sides of your fish using a sharp knife.
4. Set the fish aside and leave it in a cold place for minutes.
5. Pierce your fish all over its length using a skewer. (Better to use two skewers)
6. Your Ninja Foodi should be preheated at a temperature of about 320° F
7. Arrange the fish in the Air Crisp basket of the Ninja Foodi and press the button "Air Crisp"; then set the timer to 15 minutes
8. Make sure to turn over the fishes every 9 to 10 minutes.
9. When you see the color of the fish starting to get brown, remove your fish from the Ninja Foodi and serve it.
10. Remember that you can garnish the fish with lemon slices.
11. Enjoy your dish!

Nutrition Information

Calories: 129| Fat: 3g | Carbohydrates: 6g | Fiber: 0g |Protein: 18g

Recipe 59: Pecan Coated, Honey-Glazed Salmon

TIME TO PREPARE
6 minutes

COOK TIME
10 Minutes

SERVING
6 People

Ingredients

- 6 tbsp of Dijon mustard
- 3 tbsp of melted butter,
- 5 teaspoons of honey
- ½ Cup of bread crumbs.
- ½ Cup of chopped pecans
- 3 teaspoons of fresh chopped parsley
- 6 fillets of salmon
- A pinch of salt
- A pinch of pepper to taste

Instructions

1. Preheat your Ninja Foodi to 390° F.
2. In a large bowl, combine the mustard, the butter and the bread crumbs.
3. Add the pecans and the parsley.
4. Season each of your salmon fillets with a pinch of salt and pepper too.
5. Now, place your fillets above a greased sheet. (Baking sheet)
6. Brush the salmon with the mixture of honey and mustard.
7. Cover the top of the fillets with bread crumbs.
8. Arrange the salmon in the Air Crisp basket; then place the basket in the Ninja Foodi and sprinkle the top with bread crumbs.
9. Close the Ninja Foodi and press the button "Air Crisp"; then set the timer to about 10 minutes and the temperature to about 350° F.
10. When the time is up, serve and enjoy the salmon; after garnishing with lemon wedges!

Nutrition Information

Calories: 408.6| Fat: 16.9g | Carbohydrates: 41g | Fiber: 3.2g |Protein: 27.7g

Recipe 60: Panko Crusted Halibut

TIME TO PREPARE
8 minutes

COOK TIME
12 Minutes

SERVING
5 People

Ingredients

- ¾ Cup of Panko bread crumbs
- 1/3 Cup of chopped fresh parsley
- ¼ Cup of chopped fresh dill
- ¼ Cup of chopped fresh chives
- 1 tbsp of extra-virgin olive oil
- 1 teaspoon of finely grated lemon zest
- 1 teaspoon of sea salt
- ¼ Teaspoon of ground black pepper
- 5 halibut fillets

Instructions

1. Preheat your Ninja Foodi to 390 ° F by pressing the button SEAR/SAUTE
2. Line a baking sheet
3. In a large bowl, mix the Panko bread with the parsley
4. Add the dill, the chives, the olive oil, the lemon zest and the seas salt
5. Add the black pepper.
6. Rinse your halibut fillets and dry them using a paper towel.
7. Arrange your halibut fillets above the baking sheet.
8. Spoon the crumbs on the fish
9. Lightly press the crumb mixture on the fillet.
10. Arrange the fish fillets in your preheated Ninja Foodi Air Crisp basket
11. Set the timer to 12 minutes by pressing the button function "Air Crisp"
12. Set the temperature to 350° F.
13. Once the time is up; remove the lid; then serve the halibut and enjoy!

Nutrition Information

Calories: 273| Fat: 7g | Carbohydrates: 14g | Fiber: 0g |Protein: 38g

Recipe 61: Prawn Curry

TIME TO PREPARE
6 minutes

COOK TIME
25 Minutes

SERVING
3-4 People

Ingredients

- 10 King prawns
- 3 Cups of basmati rice
- 2 tbsp of paste of korma curry
- 1 medium finely chopped onion
- 1 and ½ cup of chicken stock
- 1 cup of frozen peas
- ½ teaspoon of coriander

Instructions

1. Rinse your basmati rice using a sieve and make sure the water runs clear.
2. Now, place your rice in a slow cooker.
3. Press the button SEAR/SAUTE
4. Sauté the onion and the korma paste in your Ninja Foodi for about 4 minutes or just until the onions become soft.
5. Scrape the onion in your Ninja Foodi together with the rice.
6. Pour in the chicken stock, then add the prawns, the peas, the coriander and cover with the lid and press the button "SLOW COOK".
7. Set the temperature to about 360°F
8. Set your timer to 25 minutes.
9. When the timer goes off, remove the lid
10. Serve and enjoy your dish.

Nutrition Information

Calories: 208.4 | Fat: 4.2g | Carbohydrates: 34.3g | Fiber: 7g | Protein: 9.3g

Recipe 62: Ninja Foodi fried Air Fried Shrimp

TIME TO PREPARE
10 minutes

COOK TIME
26 Minutes

SERVING
4 People

Ingredients

- 2/3 cup of water
- ½ teaspoon of baking powder
- 1 teaspoon of salt
- ½ cup of all-purpose flour
- ½ teaspoon of red pepper flakes
- 4 teaspoons of rice wine vinegar
- ½ cup of orange marmalade
- 2 cups of shredded sweetened coconuts
- ½ cup of bread crumbs
- 1 lb of large peeled and deveined shrimp
- Olive Oil for spraying

Instructions

For the dipping sauce:

1. Add the red pepper flakes, the vinegar, and the marmalade to your Ninja Foodi and press the button SEAR/SAUTE
2. Sauté the ingredients for about 6 minutes
3. Keep stirring until the mixture is totally combined.
4. Now, in a deep bowl, whisk all together, the salt, the flour and the baking powder.
5. Pour in the water and whisk until the mixture becomes smooth.
   Set the batter aside for around 15 minutes.
6. Now, in another bowl, toss your coconut and the breadcrumbs all together.
7. Place your shrimps into the prepared batter.
8. Now, remove your shrimps from the batter and add your coconut mixture.
9. Spray each of the shrimp on the sides with the use of oil
10. Now place the shrimps into your Air Crisp Basket
11. Close the lid of the Ninja Foodi and press the button "Air Crisp"; then set the temperature to 390°F
12. Set the timer to 5 minutes.
13. When the shrimp is cooked remove the lid of the

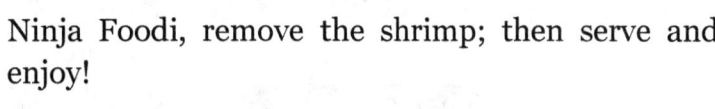

Ninja Foodi, remove the shrimp; then serve and enjoy!

Nutrition Information

Calories: 116.1| Fat: 1g | Carbohydrates: 25.2g | Fiber: 9.8g |Protein: 6.5g

Recipe 63: Bacon Wrapped shrimps

TIME TO PREPARE
4 minutes

COOK TIME
7 Minutes

SERVING
4 People

Ingredients

- 16 butter flied king shrimps
- 16 chunks of Jack cheese
- 1 of thinly sliced Serrano pepper
- 16 cooked bacon strips
- A few toothpicks
- A sauce of Barbecue

Instructions

1. Place your shrimps on a cutting board.
2. Stuff one of the shrimps using one piece of cheese and add pepper
3. Now close the shrimps and wrap it all using bacons, then secure it using a toothpick
4. Repeat the same steps with the rest of the shrimp.
5. Arrange your shrimps in the Air Crisp basket and set the temperature to 390° F
6. Close the lid of the Ninja Foodi and press the button "Air Crisp" and set the timer to 5 minutes
7. Shake the Air Crisp basket once or twice
8. If the bacon is not crunchy enough, use the oil to cook your shrimps for 2 more minutes.
9. Serve your wrapped shrimps with the barbecue sauce for dipping
10. Enjoy!

Nutrition Information

Calories: 207.6| Fat: 2g | Carbohydrates: 1g | Fiber: 0g |Protein: 23 g

Recipe 64: Octopus Chili

TIME TO PREPARE
10 minutes

COOK TIME
30 Minutes

SERVING
4-5 People

Ingredients

- 3 roots of washed coriander
- 7 medium green chillies
- 2 cloves of garlic
- 1 pinch of salt
- 2 small limes
- 1 tbsp Olive oil
- 3 lbs of octopus

Instructions

1. Mash the coriander with the help of the the mortar with the green chillies.
2. Add the 2 cloves of garlic.
3. Add 1 pinch of salt
4. Mix the ingredients very well with the sugar.
5. Add 1 teaspoon of fish sauce.
6. Pour the juice of 2 limes.
7. Add 1 teaspoon of sugar
8. Add 1 teaspoon of olive oil
9. Put the dipping sauce in a deep bowl; clean and gut the octopus
10. Cut the octopus into tentacles.
11. Place your ingredients in your Ninja Foodi and close the lid
12. Press the button "Pressure Cook" and set the timer to about 30 minutes and the temperature to 370° F
13. Make sure the valve is in sealed position and set the

pressure to High

14. When the pressure cooking cycle is over; turn off your Ninja Foodi; do a quick pressure release
15. Serve and enjoy your Octopus chili
16. Enjoy a unique, tasty dish!

Nutrition Information

Calories: 333.5| Fat: 13.8g | Carbohydrates: 22g | Fiber: 5.2g |Protein: 32.3g

Recipe 65: Rooly Poly Chinese-Style Fish

TIME TO PREPARE
8 minutes

COOK TIME
15 Minutes

SERVING
5 People

Ingredients

- 4 lb of fish
- 3 slices of Ginger
- 2 and ½ teaspoon of salt
- 4 mushrooms
- 4 teaspoons of Sugar
- 3 onions
- 4 tbsp of Soya sauce
- 2 teaspoons of Red chilli powder
- 2 tbsp of Vinegar
- 2 tbsp of Chinese winter pickle

Instructions

1. Coat the fish with the salt and set it aside for 60 minutes
2. Fill your fish with the pickle and the mushrooms
3. Cut your onions and the salads into very thin slices then spread it on your fish.
4. Now, it is time to combine your mixture with the vinegar, the stock and the soya and the sauce
5. Sprinkle your mixture on the fish
6. Place your fish in your Ninja Foodi Pressure Cooker and close the lid
7. Press the button "Pressure" and set the timer to 15 minutes and the temperature to 350° F; set the pressure to High
8. When the time is up, turn off your Ninja Foodi; then do a quick pressure release
9. Serve and enjoy your dish!

Nutrition Information

Calories: 339.5| Fat: 22.3g | Carbohydrates: 5.3g | Fiber: 0.3g |Protein: 29.9g

Recipe 66: Mahi Mahi Fish with Iceberg Leaves

TIME TO PREPARE
6 minutes

COOK TIME
15 Minutes

SERVING
4 People

Ingredients

- 6 Iceberg leaves
- 4 Fish fillets of any type you want
- 1 cup of Green coriander
- 1 pinch of Green color
- 2 Green chilli
- 1 teaspoon of Lemon juice
- 2 tbsp of water
- ¼ teaspoon of salt
- 1 pinch of Ajinomoto

Instructions

1. Preheat your Ninja Foodi to 390° F
2. Make a batter out of a pinch of salt, the lemon juice, the ajinamoto, the green chili and the green and the coriander color.
3. Rub your batter above the fish.
4. Pour 1tbsp of olive oil on the fish
5. Place the fish in the Ninja Foodi
6. Press the button "Air Crisp" and set the timer to about 15 minutes
7. When the time is up; turn off your Ninja Foodi
8. Serve your fish over the iceberg leaves
9. Enjoy an amazing dish!

Nutrition Information

Calories: 291.5| Fat: 2.7g | Carbohydrates: 28.5g | Fiber: 4.1g |Protein: 42.2g

Recipe 67: Ninja Foodi Fish and Grits

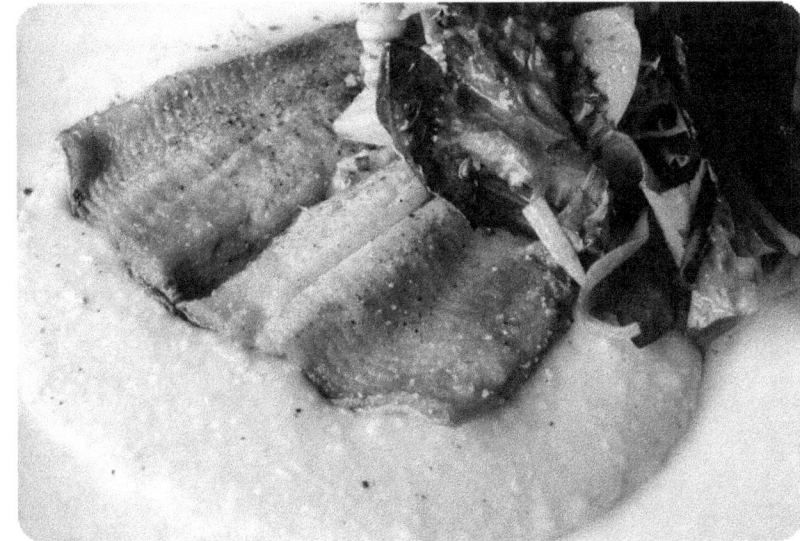

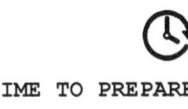

TIME TO PREPARE
6 minutes

COOK TIME
10 Minutes

SERVING
3-4 People

Ingredients

- 3 Cups of chicken broth
- 1 Cup of heavy cream
- 1 Cup of stone ground grits
- 2 Tbsp of butter
- 1 tsp of salt
- 2 pieces of tilapia fish
- 2 tsp of blackened or cajun seasoning
- vegetable oil in a spray bottle

Instructions

1. Pour the chicken broth; then add to it the heavy cream, the grits, the salt and the butter in your Ninja Foodi pressure cooker insert and stir.
2. Cover with the pressure cooker cover on and make sure the valve is set to "Seal position
3. Set the pressure to High and the timer to about 8 minutes; then when the time is up; do a Natural release for about 10 minutes
4. Press the button Cancel and release any remaining pressure by turning the valve to "Vent" position
5. In the meantime; season the fish with the blackened or the Cajun seasoning and to do that spray the fish; then rub with the seasoning into both sides of the fish
6. Once all the pressure is released, open the Ninja Foodi and stir the grits.
7. Place a piece of foil over the grits to cover it very well
8. Lay the fish over the foil and spray with the oil once again
9. Close the Air Crisp lid on the ninja Foodi and cook at a temperature of about 400°F for about 10 minutes or until the fish is easily flaked
10. Serve and enjoy!

Nutrition Information

Calories: 131.3| Fat: 2.9g | Carbohydrates: 13.1g | Fiber: 1.5g |Protein: 12.5g

Recipe 68: Ninja Foodi Fried Catfish

TIME TO PREPARE
7 minutes

COOK TIME
20 Minutes

SERVING
5 People

Ingredients

- 5 catfish filets
- 1 pinch of salt
- 1 cup of buttermilk
- 2 tbsp of hot sauce
- 2 tbsp of oil for spraying
- 1 cup of flour
- 1 cup of yellow corn
- 1 teaspoon of crab seasoning
- 1 teaspoon of garlic powder

Instructions

1. Season your catfish fillets on both of its sides with a pinch of salt and a pinch of pepper.
2. Combine all together your buttermilk with the hot sauce in a dish.
3. Add the catfish fillets and make sure that they are covered by sufficient liquid.
4. Let the ingredients soak as you prepare the rest of your ingredients
5. Prepare your baking sheet.
6. Whisk all of the ingredients, the flour, the cornmeal, the crab seasoning and the garlic powder in a different casserole
7. Remove your catfish from the quantity of buttermilk and let the excess drip off
8. Now dredge the catfish on both of its sides using the mixture of the cornmeal.
9. Place your coated fillets in a cooking pan.
10. Place the fillets in a refrigerator for around 30 minutes.
11. Place 2 of the fillets in your Ninja Foodi Air Crisp basket and drizzle with oil.

12. Set the temperature to about 390°F and the timer to 15 minutes
13. When the cooking time is complete, open the basket; then gently turn the fillets and spray your oil
14. Close the Ninja Foodi and set the timer to 5 additional minutes and the temperature to High
15. Serve and enjoy your dish!

Nutrition Information

Calories: 199| Fat: 12g | Carbohydrates: 7g | Fiber: 0.6g |Protein: 16g

Recipe 69: Crab Cakes

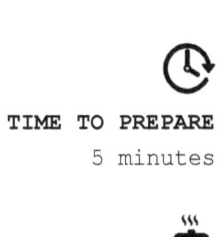

TIME TO PREPARE
5 minutes

COOK TIME
10 Minutes

SERVING
10 People

Ingredients

- 24 buttery crackers
- ½ lb of crab meat
- 1 medium minced onion
- 1 minced stalk celery
- 1 medium and minced red bell pepper
- 2 tbsp of butter
- ½ Teaspoon of crab seasoning
- 1 Teaspoon of lemon juice
- 1 Teaspoon of Cayenne pepper sauce
- 1 teaspoon of Worcestershire sauce
- 1 Beaten egg
- 1 cup of Panko bread crumbs

Instructions

1. Place your crackers in a deep bowl of a food processor
2. Finely crack and set it aside in a bowl
3. In a shallow skillet, put the butter and melt it with celery and onions with the pepper until the mixture becomes tender.
4. Remove your ingredients from the heat
5. Add your ingredients except for the Panko to the crumbs and mix it smoothly using your hand.
6. In a baking dish, put your Panko crumbs
7. Form ¼ of the mixture into a patty, and then press it into Panko while you make sure to cover both the sides and repeat the same procedure with the rest of the mixture.
8. Arrange the crab cakes in Air Crisp basket of your Ninja Foodi
9. Close the lid and press the button "Air Crisp"; then set the timer to about 10 minutes and the temperature to 390° F
10. When the timer sets off, serve and enjoy your crab cakes!
11. For the blending of the sauce, mix 1 tbsp of mayonnaise, 1tespoon of mustard and a teaspoon of ketchup.

Nutrition Information

Calories: 132| Fat: 6.4g | Carbohydrates: 0.4g | Fiber: 9.5g |Protein: 17.2g

Recipe 70: Corn and Mussels Ninja Foodi Casserole

TIME TO PREPARE
5 minutes

COOK TIME
6 Minutes

SERVING
4-5 People

Ingredients

- 1 lb of red potatoes; chopped into halves
- 4 ears of fresh corn, each snapped in half
- 12 Oz of Cajun style Andouille sausage; chopped into pieces of 2 inch each
- 4 cups of water
- 1 and ½ Tbsp of Zataran's shrimp boil liquid
- 3 tsp of old Bay seasoning, divided
- 1 lb of fresh peeled and deveined shrimp
- 1 lb of fresh mussels
- Fresh chopped parsley
- 1 Sliced lemon
- Garlic Butter for Dipping
- ½ cup of melted butter
- ½ tsp of garlic powder

Instructions

1. Add the red potatoes, the corn, the sausage, the water, the shrimp boil liquid, and about 2 tsp of old bay to your Ninja Foodi insert and stir very well.
2. Cover your Ninja Foodi with a lid and press the button "Pressure cook" on High pressure for about 4 minutes
3. Once the timer is complete, do a quick release; then open the lid once all the pressure is completely released.
4. Add the shrimp and the mussels and about 1 tsp of old bay.
5. Stir your ingredients and cover; then cook on High for about 1 minute.
6. Once the timer goes off, do a natural release for 2 minutes, then quick release any remaining pressure.
7. Combine the butter and the garlic powder in a separate medium bowl to use it as a dipping sauce.
8. Sprinkle with fresh chopped parsley; then serve and enjoy with lemon on the side

Nutrition Information

Calories: 146| Fat: 3.8g | Carbohydrates: 6.3g | Fiber: 0g |Protein: 20.2g

Recipe 71: Spicy Shrimp Fajitas

TIME TO PREPARE
7 minutes

COOK TIME
12 minutes

SERVING
5-6 People

Ingredients

- 1 Pound of medium Shrimp, with the Tail-Off
- 1 Chopped red Bell Pepper
- 1 Green, chopped bell Pepper
- ½ Cup of chopped sweet Onion
- 2 Tbsp of Fajita or Taco Seasoning
- Olive Oil Spray
- White Corn Tortillas or Flour Tortillas

Instructions

1. Spray the Air Crisp basket with olive oil spray or line with a foil.
2. Add in the shrimp, the peppers, the onion, and the seasoning to the Air Crisp basket.
3. Add in the avocado and coat with olive oil spray.
4. Mix your ingredients very well together.
5. Cook at a temperature of about 390°F for about 12 minutes using the Air Crisp button
6. Open the lid of the Ninja Foodi and spray again; then mix very well
7. Cook for about 10 additional minutes
8. Serve and enjoy on warm tortillas!

Nutrition Information

Calories: 86 | Fat: 2g | Carbohydrates: 6g | Fiber: 1g | Protein: 10g

Recipe 72: Ninja Foodi Halibut Sitka

TIME TO PREPARE
5 minutes

COOK TIME
20 Minutes

SERVING
4 People

Ingredients

- 2 lb of halibut fillet that are cut in 6 pieces.
- A pinch of salt
- A pinch of black and ground pepper
- 1 bunch of chopped green onions
- ½ Cup of mayonnaise
- ½ Cup of sour cream
- 1 Teaspoon of dried dill weed

Instructions

1. Preheat your Ninja Foodi air fryer to about 390° F
2. Season the halibut with the salt and the ground pepper.
3. In a bowl, mix all together the onions, the mayonnaise, the sour cream and the dill.
4. Now, take the halibuts and spread the mixture of onion evenly over it.
5. Place the halibut in the Air Crisp Basket and place the basket in the Ninja Foodi
6. Set your timer to a temperature of about 20 minutes and press the button "Air Crisp"
7. Cook the halibut in your Ninja Foodi until the fish becomes opaque and it flakes easily with the fork.
8. When the timer goes off, remove the Halibut from the Ninja Foodi air fryer and let it cool for 5 minutes before serving it.
9. Serve and enjoy your dish!

Nutrition Information

Calories: 404| Fat: 21g | Carbohydrates: 13g | Fiber: 0g |Protein: 37g

Recipe 73: Cedar Planked Salmon

TIME TO PREPARE
5 minutes

COOK TIME
15 Minutes

SERVING
3 People

Ingredients

- 4 untreated cedar planks
- 1/3 cup of vegetable oil
- 1 and ½ tbsp of rice vinegar
- 1 teaspoon of sesame oil
- 1/3 cup of soy sauce
- ¼ Cup of large and chopped green onions
- 1 Tbsp of grated and fresh ginger root
- 1 teaspoon of minced garlic
- 2 lb of salmon fillets with its skin removed

Instructions

1. Start by soaking the cedar planks for 1 hour in a quantity of warm water.
2. Soak the cedar planks longer if you can; the longer the better.
3. Now take a shallow dish and stir in the vegetable oil, the rice vinegar, the sesame oil, the soy sauce and the green onions together with ginger.
4. Put your salmon fillets in the prepared marinade.
5. Cover the salmon fillets and marinate it for at least 20 minutes.
6. Preheat you Ninja Foodi on a medium heat.
7. Place your planks in the Air Crisp basket of the Ninja Foodi
8. Cook the salmon fillets for about 15 minutes and over a temperature of 360°F by using the setting button "Air Crisp"
9. Once perfectly cooked; serve and enjoy your salmon fillets.

Nutrition Information

Calories: 664| Fat: 42g | Carbohydrates: 18g | Fiber: 8g |Protein: 49g

Recipe 74: Crab Leg Ninja Foodi Pot

TIME TO PREPARE
3 minutes

COOK TIME
7 Minutes

SERVING
3 People

Ingredients

- 5 Crab Leg clusters
- 2 Tablespoons of chopped or minced garlic
- 1 Tablespoon of Tony Chachere's seasoning
- 1 Cup of water
- 1 Sliced lemon

Instructions

1. Place a trivet in your Ninja Foodi
2. Pour the water into the Ninja Foodi; then add the garlic to the Ninja foodi Pot
3. Add the Tony Chachere's seasoning
4. Place in the sliced lemons on the trivet
5. Add the crab legs to the Ninja Foodi
6. Close the lid and move the valve to the "seal" position
7. Cook on high pressure for about 2 minutes
8. When the timer beeps; move the seal to "release" position; then quick release all the pressure
9. Once the pressure is completely released; remove the lid
10. Let the Crab Legs continue to steam in your Ninja Foodi for about 5 minutes
11. Serve with the melted butter and enjoy your seafood dish!

Nutrition Information

Calories: 440| Fat: 34g | Carbohydrates: 2g | Fiber: 0g |Protein: 32g

Recipe 75: Bang Bang Shrimp

TIME TO PREPARE
4 minutes

COOK TIME
10 Minutes

SERVING
3-4 People

Ingredients

- ½ cup of All purpose flour
- 2 Large Eggs
- 1 Cup of fine breadcrumbs
- 2 tbsp of Grapeseed oil
- 1 tsp of Garlic powder
- ½ tsp of Kosher salt
- ½ tsp of ground Black pepper
- 1 lb of uncooked large shrimp
- ⅓ cup of Mayonnaise
- ⅓ cup of Sweet and

Instructions

1. Using three bowls, set a dipping station; then in the first bowl; add in the first bowl, add in the flour; in the second bowl, add in the eggs and in the third bowl, the breadcrumbs , the Blair powder, the oil, the salt and the pepper
2. Coat the shrimp into the flour and shake off any excess; then dip in the egg.
3. Roll into the mixture of the breadcrumb.
4. Preheat your Foodi to a temperature of 400°F and set the timer for about 5 minutes.
5. Once preheated and the 5 minutes are complete, open the lid; then add in the shrimp in one layer to the Air Crisp Basket
6. Set the button "Air Crisp" and the temperature to 400° for about 10 minutes, using the cook and Crisp Insert

- spicy Thai chili sauce
- 1 tbsp of Sriracha sauce
- 1 tbsp of Lime juice
- 2 tsp of Honey
- 1 Pinch of kosher salt

6. and repeat the same process with the rest of the batches
7. While the shrimp is being cooked; prepare the sauce; whisk all together the mayonnaise, the sweet and spicy Thai chili sauce, the sriracha sauce, the lime juice and the honey.
8. Make sure they are well combined; then add the salt to taste
9. When the shrimp are finished cooking, drizzle some quantity of sauce over the shrimp
10. Drizzle some quantity of sauce over the shrimp; then serve and enjoy your dish

Nutrition Information

Calories: 331| Fat: 21g | Carbohydrates: 20g | Fiber: 1.1g |Protein: 15g

Recipe 76: Ninja Foodi Panko Crusted Cod with Quinoa

TIME TO PREPARE
10 minutes

COOK TIME
15 Minutes

SERVING
3 People

Ingredients

- ½ Pound of white quinoa
- 1 and ½ tsp of fine sea salt, divided
- 410ml of water, divided
- 1 Cup of panko bread crumbs
- 1 Cup of unsalted butter, melted
- Fresh chopped parsley
- The Zest and the juice of 2 lemons
- 4 fresh cod fillets
- 1 Bunch of asparagus, with the stems trimmed
- 1 tsp of extra virgin

Instructions

1. Place the quinoa with 1 teaspoon of salt, and about 350ml of water into the Ninja Foodi pot and close the lid
2. Make sure the pressure release valve is in the SEAL position.
3. Select the button function PRESSURE and set it to HIGH; then set the time to about 2 minutes.
4. Select the button START/STOP to start and while the quinoa is cooking, place the breadcrumbs in a large bowl and stir very well
5. Add in the parsley, the lemon zest and the juice; then add in 1 teaspoon of salt.
6. Press the Panko mixture evenly on top of each of the cod fillets
7. When the pressure cooking cycle is complete, do a quick pressure release and move the valve to the VENT position; then carefully remove the lid
8. Add the remaining 60ml of water to the quinoa
9. Toss the oil with the asparagus and 1 teaspoon

olive oil

of salt

10. Lay the asparagus on top of the quinoa
11. Place a reversible Rack in the Ninja foodi and the pot over the Quinoa and the asparagus
12. Place the cod fillets over the rack with the breading side up
13. Close the crisping lid; and select the button BAKE/ ROAST; then set the temperature to about 360°F and set the timer to about 12 minutes
14. Select the button START/STOP to start; then cook for about 2 additional minutes
15. Serve and enjoy your dish with the cooked Quinoa!

Nutrition Information

Calories: 297| Fat: 3.8g | Carbohydrates: 32.4g | Fiber: 3.1g |Protein: 31.6g

Recipe 77: Ninja Foodi Mackerels

TIME TO PREPARE
5 minutes

COOK TIME
6 Minutes

SERVING
3 People

Ingredients

- 2 Mackerel fillet
- Olive oil
- Salted Kelp Tea
- 1 Cup of rice
- Seaweed and leaves for garnish
- 1 Pinch of salt

Instructions

1. Cook the rice in a rice cooker.
2. Pat the mackerel dry and sprinkle with 1 pinch of salt and set aside for about 20 minutes.
3. Pour 1 cup of water in your Ninja Foodi and place a trivet in it; then cut the mackerel into small pieces
4. Make Onigiri by shaping it around the fish with a cling wrap
5. Arrange the fish in the Air Crisp Basket of the Ninja Foodi and press the setting button "Air Crisp"; then set the timer for about 6 minutes
6. Boil the water and make the salted kelp tea
7. When the timer of the Ninja Foodi is done, remove from the Ninja Foodi; then garnish and serve in a bowl with the kelp tea
8. Enjoy your dish!

Nutrition Information

Calories: 158| Fat: 9g | Carbohydrates: 0g | Fiber: 0g |Protein: 23g

CHAPTER 6: POULTRY RECIPES

Recipe 78: Southern-style chicken

TIME TO PREPARE
5 minutes

COOK TIME
10 Minutes

SERVING
6 People

Ingredients

- 3 Pounds of chicken leg quarters
- 1 Teaspoon of salt
- 1 Teaspoon of pepper
- 1 Teaspoon of garlic powder
- 1 Teaspoon of paprika
- 1 Cup of coconut flour
- 2 Tbsp of olive oil

Instructions

1. In a deep and large bowl, combine altogether the chicken, the salt, the pepper, the garlic powder, and the paprika.
2. With clean hands; rub the chicken meat with spices and make sure it is very-well coated.
3. Cover the chicken and refrigerate it for about 2 hours.
4. Preheat your Ninja Foodi to a temperature of about 350° F
5. In a medium bowl, add your coconut flour to the chicken and toss it very well together to evenly coat it
6. Add the coconut flour to the seasoned chicken and toss well to coat.
7. Arrange the chicken meat into the Air Crisp basket and slide the basket in the Ninja Foodi; then close the lid
8. Press the button "Air Crisp" and set the timer to about 10 minutes and the heat to 370° F
9. When the timer beeps; remove the chicken from the N inja Foodi
10. Serve and enjoy!

Nutrition Information

Calories: 472.1| Fat: 30g | Carbohydrates: 11g | Fiber: 2g |Protein: 2g

Recipe 79: Stuffed Chicken with Tomato Sauce

TIME TO PREPARE
10 minutes

COOK TIME
30 Minutes

SERVING
4 People

Ingredients

- 4 Boneless, pounded and skinless chicken breasts
- 14 Oz of diced tomatoes
- ¼ Cup of pesto
- 6 slices of sliced Provolone Cheese
- 1 Cup of Italian style bread crumbs

Instructions

1. Preheat your Ninja Foodi to a temperature of about 390° F.
2. Lay the pounded chicken on a cutting surface and toss 1 tablespoon of pesto over each of the chicken pieces
3. Put pieces of cheese on top of the pesto
4. Spoon about 1 tablespoon of the canned tomatoes and roll the chicken; then secure it with a tooth pick
5. Pour the remaining quantity of tomatoes right into the bottom of the Ninja Foodi
6. Roll the pieces of the chicken through the breadcrumbs.
7. Arrange the stuffed chicken into the tomatoes and spray the chicken with a non-stick spray.
8. Close he lid of your Ninja Foodi and set the timer to about 30 minutes and the temperature to about 375° F by pressing the button Pressure Cook
9. Set the pressure to High and when the timer beeps, remove the chicken from the heat; then serve and enjoy your chicken dish!

Nutrition Information

Calories: 104.4| Fat: 5g | Carbohydrates: 15.1g | Fiber: 4.8g |Protein: 2.4g

Recipe 80: Asian-Style Chicken

TIME TO PREPARE
6 minutes

COOK TIME
18 Minutes

SERVING
3-4 People

Ingredients

- 1 Cup of coconut Milk
- 1 Cup of fresh Lime Juice
- 1/2 Cup of Rice Wine Vinegar
- 2 Tablespoons of Fish Sauce
- 3 Finely minced green onions
- 2 Finely sliced garlic cloves
- 2 Teaspoons of finely minced fresh ginger
- 1 Tablespoon of Hot Sauce
- 1 Tablespoon of finely minced cilantro
- 7 Chicken Breasts
- ½ Teaspoon of salt and 1 teaspoon of ground pepper
- Slices of lime Slices for garnishing
- Sliced fresh green

Instructions

1. Preheat your Ninja Foodi to about 375° degrees Fahrenheit by pressing the button Function "SEAR/SAUTE"
2. Combine the coconut milk, the lime juice, the rice wine vinegar, the fish sauce, the green onions, the garlic, the ginger, the hot sauce, and the cilantro into a medium bowl and combine very well
3. Season the chicken meat with pepper and salt
4. Place the chicken into a plastic bag and pour half of your marinade over the chicken.
5. Seal the bag and set the chicken aside for about 30 minutes
6. Add the remaining quantity of the marinade to a pot over a medium high heat
7. Boil the chicken with the marinade until the consistency of the glaze is reduced
8. Remove the chicken from the marinade and rub it with the glaze
9. Put the chicken with its skin side down in the Air Crisp basket of the Ninja Foodi
10. Slide the Air Crisp basket in your Ninja Foodi
11. Close the lid of the Ninja Foodi and set the timer to about 18 minutes and the temperature to 365° F by pressing the button "Air Crisp"

Onions

12. Once the timer beeps, remove the chicken from the Ninja Foodi
13. Serve and enjoy your chicken with green onions and lemon wedges!

Nutrition Information

Calories: 329| Fat: 14.33g | Carbohydrates: 22.17g | Fiber: 2.1g |Protein: 27.16g

Recipe 81: Broccoli with Sesame Chicken

TIME TO PREPARE
10 minutes

COOK TIME
25 Minutes

SERVING
3 People

Ingredients

- 2 Cups of broccoli florets
- 1 Egg white
- 2 Tablespoons of cornstarch
- ½ Teaspoon of sea salt
- 1 Pound of boneless and skinless chicken breasts
- 2 Tablespoons of vegetable oil
- 1 Seeded and cut red pepper
- 2 Thinly sliced scallions
- 1 Minced garlic clove
- 3 Tablespoons of gluten-free tamari
- 1 Teaspoon of sesame oil
- 3 Tablespoons of honey
- 2 Tablespoons of sesame seeds

Instructions

1. In a large pot; put the broccoli florets into the water and let simmer for about 15 minutes; add a little bit of curcuma
2. When the broccoli florets become tender, turn off the heat and sprinkle a little bit of salt
3. Remove the broccoli and drain it into a colander; then rinse it very well and set it aside for about 5 minutes to cool. In the meantime, mix the egg white with the cornstarch and the salt into a deep bowl
4. Add the meat of chicken; then toss the ingredients very well to combine it.
5. Heat about 1 tablespoon of coconut oil to the mixture
6. Preheat your Ninja Foodi to about 350° F
7. Arrange the chicken meat in the Air Crisp basket of the Ninja Foodi and close the lid
8. Press the button "Air Crisp" and set the timer to about 10 minutes
9. When the timer beeps, remove the chicken from the Ninja Foodi basket and set it aside; then put the pepper and the scallions into the basket and close the lid again and set the temperature to 325° F and the timer to 5 minutes

- 1 Teaspoon of curcuma

10. When the timer beeps, remove the pepper and the scallions from the Ninja Foodi and put all of your ingredients into a medium saucepan
11. Add your chicken to the pot; then add the tamari, the sesame oil and let the ingredients simmer for about 2 minutes
12. Add the broccoli and the green scallions; then serve your dish hot
13. Enjoy your dish!

Nutrition Information

Calories: 365| Fat: 14g | Carbohydrates: 21g | Fiber: 4g |Protein: 39g

Recipe 82: Chicken with Garlic and Mushrooms

TIME TO PREPARE

5 minutes

COOK TIME

20 Minutes

SERVING

4 People

Ingredients

- 2 Pounds of chicken pieces
- ½ Teaspoon of dried thyme
- ½ Teaspoon of salt
- ½ Teaspoon of pepper
- 5 Tablespoons of olive oil
- ¼ Cup of butter

To prepare the sauce:

- 5 Minced garlic cloves
- 2 Medium chopped onions
- ½ Cup of dry sherry
- 3 Tablespoons of tomato paste
- 1 Pinch of dried basil
- 2 Tablespoons of white wine vinegar
- 1 Teaspoon of sugar

Instructions

1. Season the chicken with the salt, the pepper and the thyme.
2. Put the chicken in the Air Crisp basket of a Ninja Foodi fryer and drizzle it with oil on all its sides
3. Close the lid of the Ninja Foodi and press the button "Air Crisp"; then set the timer to 12 minutes; meanwhile, prepare the sauce
   a medium saucepan over a medium heat and add the garlic to it; add the onions and pour 2 tablespoons of olive oil and sauté the ingredients for about 3 minutes
4. Add the remaining ingredients except for the mushrooms; pour 1 cup of water and let the ingredients boil.
5. When the timer of the Ninja Foodi beeps, remove the chicken from it; then place over the prepared sauce
6. Serve and enjoy your dish with thyme and basil!

- 1 Teaspoon of mustard
- 4 Large chopped tomatoes
- 3 Cups of sliced mushrooms
- Basil leaves and thyme leaves for garnishing

Nutrition Information

Calories: 160| Fat: 11g | Carbohydrates: 8g | Fiber: 0g | Protein: 7g

Recipe 83: Chicken Breast with mustard and herbs

TIME TO PREPARE
7 minutes

COOK TIME
30 Minutes

SERVING
5 People

Ingredients

- 2 Teaspoons of olive oil
- 5 Chicken breasts
- 1 Teaspoon of dried thyme
- ½ Teaspoon of dried sage
- ½ Teaspoon of smoked paprika
- 1 Teaspoon of salt
- ½ Teaspoon of freshly ground black pepper
- ¼ Cup of maple syrup
- 2 Tablespoon of Dijon mustard
- 1 Tablespoon of butter

Instructions

1. Pre heat your Ninja Foodie to a temperature of about 350°F.
2. Rub the chicken breasts with the olive oil
3. Brush the chicken with a mixture of sage, the paprika, the thyme and the pepper
4. Transfer your seasoned chicken breast to the Air Crisp basket of your Ninja Foodi
5. Close the lid of the Ninja Foodi and set the temperature to about 350°F and the timer to about 10 minutes.
6. Turn the chicken breasts once or twice and cook it for 10 additional minutes. Meanwhile, mix the mustard; the maple syrup; then add the butter to your ingredients and stir very well. Put the ingredients in a small saucepan over a medium heat for about 3 minutes
7. When the timer of the Ninja Foodi beeps, remove the chicken breasts from it and rub the glaze on the chicken breasts
8. Air Crisp the chicken breasts for about 4 additional minutes
9. Once the timer beeps, serve and enjoy your chicken.

Nutrition Information

Calories: 271.5| Fat: 6.9g | Carbohydrates: 32g | Fiber: 3.3g |Protein: 18.2g

Recipe 84: Honey-Glazed Chicken wings

TIME TO PREPARE
8 minutes

COOK TIME
40 Minutes

SERVING
4 People

Ingredients

- 15 Pieces of Chicken Wings
- ¾ Cup of Potato Starch
- ¼ Cup of Clover Honey
- 1/4 cup of butter
- 4 Tablespoons of Fresh minced Garlic
    ½ Teaspoon of Kosher Salt

Instructions

1. Start by rinsing and drying your chicken wings
2. Put the potato starch in a large bowl and coat the chicken wings with it
3. Arrange the chicken wings in the Air Crisp basket of your Ninja Foodi and close the lid
4. Set the timer to about 20 minutes and the temperature to 375° F using the button
5. Make sure to shake the Air Crisp basket of the Ninja Foodi each 4 to 5 minutes.
6. When the timer beeps; remove the chicken wings from the Ninja Foodi
7. Put a medium pot over the stove and set the heat to low
8. Add the butter to the pot and add the garlic
9. Sauté the crushed garlic for about 4 minutes
10. Add the honey and the salt and let simmer for around 22 minutes; make sure to stir from time to time
11. Arrange the chicken wings in a serving platter and pour the honey sauce over it
12. Serve and enjoy your delicious dish!

Nutrition Information

Calories: 284.7| Fat: 15g | Carbohydrates: 7.8g | Fiber: 0.5g |Protein: 27.6g

Recipe 85: Chicken Nuggets with Mayonnaise

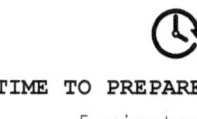

TIME TO PREPARE
5 minutes

COOK TIME
8 Minutes

SERVING
5 People

Ingredients

- 3 Medium breasts of Chicken
- ¼ Cup of Mayonnaise
- 1 Teaspoon of white vinegar
- 1 Cup of Almond flour
- ½ Teaspoon of sca salt
- ¼ Teaspoon of black pepper
- 2 Tablespoons of olive oil

Instructions

1. Fill in a deep and large bowl with the water and add to it a little bit of salt
2. Put the chicken into the salty water and set it aside to brine for about 15 minutes
3. Drain the chicken and pat it dry with paper towels
4. Cut the chicken meat into the size of nuggets
5. In a medium bowl, whisk altogether the vinegar and the mayonnaise. In a separate bowl, combine the almond flour and a little bit of salt; then add a dash of black pepper
6. Coat the chicken pieces with the mayonnaise and press it into the mixture of the almond flour
7. Preheat your Ninja Foodi to around 350° F by pressing the button Air Crisp
8. Arrange the chicken nuggets in the basket of the Ninja Foodi and drizzle with a little bit of oil; then close the lid
9. Set the timer to about 8 minutes
10. When the timer beeps; remove the chicken from the Ninja Foodi; then serve and enjoy your dish!

Nutrition Information

Calories: 491| Fat: 33g | Carbohydrates: 24g | Fiber: 1.4g |Protein: 25g

Recipe 86: Chicken Pakora

TIME TO PREPARE
5 minutes

COOK TIME
30 Minutes

SERVING
7 People

Ingredients

- 1 Pound of diced chicken
- ½ Finely chopped small cabbage
- 2 Grated carrots
- ½ Teaspoon of ground turmeric
- ½ Teaspoon of chili powder
- ½ Teaspoon of ground coriander
- ½ Teaspoon of ground cumin
- ½ Teaspoon of Tandoori Masala powder
- ½ Teaspoon of salt
- 1 handful of chopped fresh coriander
- 5 Tablespoons of almond flour
- Basil leaves

Instructions

1. Combine altogether the chicken, the cabbage and the carrots. Season the chicken with the turmeric, the chili powder, the ground coriander, the cumin, the Tandoori Masala, the salt and the fresh coriander.
2. Add the almond flour to water and make a kind of heavy mixture
3. Mix your ingredients very well
4. Preheat your Ninja Foodi to a temperature of about 350° F
5. Arrange the chicken in Air Crisp basket of the Ninja Foodi
6. Close the lid of your Ninja Foodi and press the setting button "Air Crisp" and set the timer to about 11 minutes
7. When the timer beeps, remove the chicken from the Ninja Foodi, then serve and enjoy it!

Nutrition Information

Calories: 157| Fat: 4.9g | Carbohydrates: 9.4g | Fiber: 1.2g |Protein: 18.1g

Recipe 87: Cashew Chicken

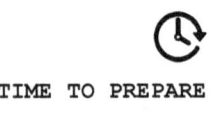

TIME TO PREPARE
6 minutes

COOK TIME
30 Minutes

SERVING
5 People

Ingredients

- 2 Cups of cashew nuts
- 1 Teaspoon of Ghee
- 1 Teaspoon of coriander powder
- 1 Teaspoon of red chili powder
- ½ Teaspoon of Garam Masala powder
- ½ Teaspoon of black pepper powder
- 1 Teaspoon of Black salt
- ½ Teaspoon of salt
- 2 Teaspoons of fry mango powder
- 1 Pound of boneless and skinless chicken breast

Instructions

1. Chop the chicken into small pieces
2. Combine all of your ingredients into a large mixing bowl and mix it very well
3. Line your ingredients into the Air Crisp basket of your Ninja Foodi and combine it very well
4. Set your Ninja Foodi to a temperature of about 340 degrees Fahrenheit using the button function "Air Crisp" and set the timer to 12 minutes
5. When the timer beeps, remove the chicken from the Ninja Foodi and let it rest for about 5 minutes
6. Serve and enjoy your chicken with cashews!

Nutrition Information

Calories: 273.9| Fat: 9.1g | Carbohydrates: 16.4g | Fiber: 2.6g |Protein: 31g

Recipe 88: Spicy Buffalo Chicken

TIME TO PREPARE
8 minutes

COOK TIME
20 Minutes

SERVING
5 People

Ingredients

- ½ fowl or chicken
- 2 quarts of chicken broth
- ¼ Cup of coarsely chopped onion
- ½ Cup of coarsely chopped carrots
- ½ Cup of coarsely chopped celery
- 1 Teaspoon of saffron threads
- ¾ Cup of corn kernels
- ½ Cup of finely chopped celery
- 1 tablespoon of fresh chopped parsley
- 1 Cup of cooked egg noodles

Instructions

1. Preheat your Ninja Foodi to a degree of 350° F
2. Combine the garlic powder, the paprika, the chili powder and the black pepper into a medium deep bowl.
3. Season the chicken with the spices and toss it very well
4. Arrange the chicken in the basket of Ninja Foodi and close the lid
5. Press the button "Air Crisp" and set the timer to about 6 minutes and the temperature to around 350° F
6. When the timer beeps, remove the chicken from the Ninja Foodi; then transfer it to a serving dish
7. Pour the sauce over your chicken
8. Serve and enjoy your delicious dish!

Nutrition Information

Calories: 176| Fat: 4g | Carbohydrates: 5g | Fiber: 2 g |Protein: 6g

Recipe 89: Chicken with Prunes and Olives

TIME TO PREPARE
6 minutes

COOK TIME
20 Minutes

SERVING
3 People

Ingredients

- 3 Minced garlic cloves
- 1/3 Cup of pitted prunes
- 9 green olives
- 2 tbsp of capers
- 2 tbsp of olive oil
- 2 tbsp of red wine vinegar
- 3 bay leaves
- 1 tbsp of dried oregano
- 1 pinch of salt
- 1 Pinch of ground pepper
- 3 lb of chicken (Have their skin removed and cut it into pieces)
- ¼ Cup of packed brown sugar
- ¼ Cup of dry white wine

Instructions

1. In a deep bowl mix your prunes, the garlic, the olives, the capers, the olive oil, the vinegar, the bay leaves, the oregano, the salt and the pepper.
2. Combine the ingredients together very well.
3. Now, in a baking tray, spread your mixture tight in the bottom.
4. Add your chicken pieces
5. Keep stirring and cover the chicken in the fridge for the entire night.
6. When you are ready to cook your chicken, preheat your Ninja Foodi to a temperature of about 350 ° F.
7. Sprinkle a little bit of brown sugar on the top of the chicken.
8. Pressure cook the chicken in your preheated Ninja Foodi for 20 minutes using the button "Pressure Cook" and set the pressure to High
9. After the timer sets off; the timer beeps; do a quick release pressure method
10. Garnish with finely chopped fresh parsley and pour juices of your choice above the surface.
11. Serve and enjoy your dish!

- For garnish, use 1 tbsp of chopped and fresh parsley

Nutrition Information

Calories: 331.2| Fat: 12.2g | Carbohydrates: 27.9g | Fiber: 1.8g |Protein: 27.8g

Recipe 90: Chicken Chutney

TIME TO PREPARE
5 minutes

COOK TIME
10 Minutes

SERVING
3-4 People

Ingredients

- 1 Pound of Boneless and cubed Chicken
- 2 Tablespoons of cumin
- 2 Tablespoons of Coriander seeds
- 8 Black Peppercorns 6-8
- 3 Whole garlic cloves
- Fresh Coriander
- 2 Seeded Green chilies
- ½ Cup of mint leaves
- 1 Tablespoon of grated ginger
- 1 Tablespoon of crushed garlic
- 1 Cup of yoghurt
- 1 Teaspoon of Garam Masala
- 1 tablespoon of Ghee

Instructions

1. Start by dry roasting the cumin seeds, the coriander seeds, the peppercorns and the cloves
2. Grind your ingredients; then chop the coriander and the mint leaves; then cut the green chilies
3. Mix your greens with the ground Masala to make a paste
4. In a mixing bowl, combine the yogurt with the salt and the Garam Masala
5. Season the chicken with salt, the pepper; and a little bit of oil or ghee
6. Set the chicken meat aside for about 60 minutes
7. Arrange the chicken meat in the Air Crisp basket of your Ninja Foodi and close the lid
8. Set the timer to about 10 minutes and the temperature to 360° F using the button "Air Crisp"
9. When the timer beeps, remove the chicken from the Ninja Foodi; then transfer it to a saucepan on a medium – high heat with the ghee and add the chutney paste Sauté your ingredients for about 4

- 1 Pinch of salt
- 1 Sliced lemon

minutes

10. Serve and enjoy with slices of lemon!

Nutrition Information

Calories: 263| Fat: 2g | Carbohydrates: 25g | Fiber: 0g |Protein: 23g

Recipe 91: Chicken Potato Nests

TIME TO PREPARE
8 minutes

COOK TIME
15 Minutes

SERVING
3 People

| Ingredients | Instructions |

- 3 to 4 large Potatoes
- 1 Teaspoon of salt
- ½ Pound of shredded or finely cut cooked chicken
- ½ Teaspoon of pepper
- 2 and ½ teaspoon of garlic powder
- 2 and ½ teaspoons of onion powder
- 4 Teaspoons of vegetable oil
- 2 Tablespoons of cooking spray
- 4 Cups of thawed spinach thawed
- 4 Tablespoons of extra virgin olive oil
- 4 Beaten eggs

1. Preheat your Ninja Foodi to about 390° F
2. Start by grating the potatoes; then add 1 pinch of salt and combine the ingredients very well; then set it aside into a colander and put a bowl under the colander for about 15 minutes
3. Into a large non-stick skillet; sauté the shredded chicken and the spinach into 1 tablespoon of olive oil
4. Season with 2 teaspoons of garlic powder and 2 teaspoons of onion powder
5. Add a little bit of salt and sauté for about 4 minutes and when it is done, set it aside
6. Season your ingredients with ½ teaspoon of garlic powder and ½ teaspoon of onion powder
7. Add ½ teaspoon of pepper and pour in 4 teaspoons of vegetable oil; then mix very well.
8. Arrange the grated potatoes into the muffin cups and press it into the bottom.
9. In a small and deep bowl, mix the eggs with a little bit of salt; then add the spinach and the shredded chicken

10. Put the potatoes in each of the nests
11. Place your muffin cups in the Air Crisp basket of the Ninja Foodi Air Crisp basket and close the lid
12. Set the timer for about 15 minutes and the temperature to 350° F using the button "Air Crisp"
13. When the timer beeps, remove the muffin tin from the Air Crisp basket and set it aside for about 10 minutes to cool down
14. Remove from the Ninja Foodi; then serve and enjoy your chicken cups!

Nutrition Information

Calories: 128.8| Fat: 5.5g | Carbohydrates: 1.1g | Fiber: 0.2g |Protein: 17.7g

Recipe 92: Chicken Liver and cauliflower Bites

TIME TO PREPARE
10 minutes

COOK TIME
20 Minutes

SERVING
8 People

Ingredients

- 1 Pound of organic cauliflower
- ½ Pound of chicken liver
- 1 Teaspoon of unrefined sea salt
- 2 Tablespoons of organic butter
- 3 Eggs
- 1/3 Cup of coconut flour

Instructions

1. Start by cooking the cauliflower into boiling water until it becomes tender, for about 8 minutes
2. Drain the cauliflower and set it aside
3. Preheat your Ninja Foodi to about 350 °F by pressing the button "SEAR/SAUTE"
4. Add the coconut oil; the chicken liver and a little bit of salt to the purée of the cauliflower and crack in the eggs; then whisk very well until your ingredients are completely combined
5. Sift in the coconut flour and mix very well; then set the mixture aside for about 10 minutes
6. Let the mixture stand for 10 minutes.
7. Prepare a baking sheet and line it with a baking paper
8. Prepare a small pastry bag that has quite a large star tip
9. Start piping the cauliflower rosette over the parchment paper
10. Arrange your duchess cauliflowers on a greased baking sheet in the Air Crisp basket of your Ninja Foodi and close the lid
11. Press the button " Bake/ Roast"; then set the timer to about 20 minutes
12. When the timer beeps, remove the cauliflower bites

13. Serve and enjoy your delicious chicken bites!

Nutrition Information

Calories: 128.4| Fat: 2.6g | Carbohydrates: 22.9g | Fiber: 3g |Protein: 4.7g

Recipe 93: Chicken Salad

TIME TO PREPARE
6 minutes

COOK TIME
10 Minutes

SERVING
3-4 People

Ingredients

- 2 Pounds of potatoes
- 1 Bunch of trimmed and sliced asparagus
- 4 Coarsely chopped bacon rashers
- ½ Cup of mayonnaise
- ¼ Cup of sour cream
- 2 Tablespoons of lemon juice
- 3 Teaspoons of Dijon mustard
- 1 Tablespoon of coarsely chopped tarragon
- ½ Pound of shredded chicken
- 4 Thinly sliced green onions

Instructions

1. Put your potatoes into a saucepan over a medium heat and cover it with 2 and ½ cups of water
2. Let the potato boil for about 10 minutes
3. Drain the potatoes and cut it into small dices
4. Season the potatoes with a little bit of salt and pepper
5. Toss the potatoes in the Air Crisp basket of the Ninja Foodi and add the shredded chicken and the asparagus
6. Drizzle with 1 tablespoon of olive oil and close the lid
7. Press the button "Air Crisp" and set the timer to about 12 minutes and the temperature to 350° F
8. When the timer beeps, remove the ingredients from the Ninja Foodi and transfer it to a deep bowl
9. Add the mayonnaise, the sour cream, the lemon juice, the mustard and the tarragon
10. Season with a pinch of salt and 1 pinch of pepper
11. Add the onions and top with mayonnaise
12. Serve and enjoy your delicious salad
13. Serve and enjoy your chicken salad!

Nutrition Information

Calories: 254| Fat: 18g | Carbohydrates: 3.3g | Fiber: 0.4g |Protein: 19g

Recipe 94: Chicken Quinoa Salad

TIME TO PREPARE
6 minutes

COOK TIME
22 Minutes

SERVING
3 People

Ingredients

- ½ Pound of raw chicken breast
- ½ Cup of uncooked quinoa
- 1 Medium chopped tomato
- 1 Sliced spring onion
- ½ Sliced medium cucumber
- ½ Cup of walnuts
- 1 Tablespoon of rocket leaves
- ¼ Chopped fresh mint
- 1 Tablespoon of fresh lime juice
- ½ Tablespoon of fresh orange juice
- ½ Tablespoon of olive oil
- 1 Tablespoon of vinegar
- 1 Teaspoon of Dijon mustard

Instructions

1. Put the quinoa with 1 cup of water into a deep saucepan over a medium-high heat and let it boil for about 12 minutes
2. Fluff the quinoa with a fork and set it aside for about 10 minutes
3. Finely chop the chicken and season it with a pinch of salt and pepper
4. Preheat your Ninja Foodi to 365° F and arrange the chicken in the Air Crisp Basket of the Ninja Foodi and close the lid
5. Set the timer to about 10 minutes using the button "Air Crisp"
6. When the timer beeps, remove the chicken from the Ninja Foodi and prepare the dressing by mixing the spring onion with the tomato, the cucumber, the walnuts, the rocket leaves, the mint and the cooked quinoa.
7. Toss your ingredients very well
8. Pour the dressing over the salad and mix very well
9. Serve and enjoy your salad on a serving platter and top it with the chicken!

Nutrition Information

Calories: 241.8| Fat: 5.7g | Carbohydrates: 29.8g | Fiber: 4.5g |Protein: 19g

Recipe 95: Ninja Foodi Chicken casserole

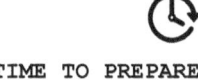

TIME TO PREPARE
10 minutes

COOK TIME
25 Minutes

SERVING
3-4 People

Ingredients

- 2 Minced garlic cloves
- ½ Cup of diced onion
- 1 Diced red pepper
- 2 Stripped and cut bacon
- 1 Pound of diced chicken
- 1 Spiralized sweet potato
- 2 Cups of spinach
- ½ Cup of water or broth
- 1 Teaspoon of paprika
- ½ Teaspoon of Cayenne
- 1 Teaspoon of salt-free all-purpose seasoning
- 6 Beaten eggs

Instructions

1. Preheat your Ninja Foodi to about 350° Fahrenheit using the button "SEAR/SAUTE"
2. sauté the garlic, the onion, the peppers, the bacon, the chicken and the sweet potato until the chicken is cooked very well
3. Add the spinach, the water and the seasonings; then cook for about 5 minutes
4. Meanwhile; combine the eggs in a deep bowl and pour it over your mixture
5. Close the lid of the Ninja Foodi and set the timer to 20 minutes
6. and the temperature to about 370°F using the button "Pressure Cook"
7. Make sure the valve is in sealed position
8. When the timer beeps; do a quick release pressure
9. Serve and enjoy your dish!

Nutrition Information

Calories: 235| Fat: 8.2g | Carbohydrates: 17.4g | Fiber: 2.9g |Protein: 22.8g

Recipe 96: Greek-Style CHICKEN

TIME TO PREPARE
7 minutes

COOK TIME
20 Minutes

SERVING
3-4 People

Ingredients

- ½ Cup of olive oil
- 3 chopped cloves of garlic
- 1tbsp of fresh rosemary
- 1 tbsp of fresh thyme (Finely chopped)
- 1 tbsp of chopped fresh oregano
- 2 large lemon
- 3lb of chicken that are cut into pieces
- Salt
- Black pepper

Instructions

1. In a large bowl, combine altogether the cloves of garlic, the prunes, the olives, the capers, the olive oil, the vinegar, the bay leaves, the oregano, the salt and the pepper.
2. Mix the ingredients very well.
3. Now, add the chicken and rub the mixture very well over it
4. Now, place the chicken in the refrigerator for 12 hours
5. Remove the chicken from the refrigerator; then place your ingredients in your Ninja Foodi Pressure cooker insert
6. Sprinkle a little bit of brown sugar on the top of the chicken then pour the white wine above the chicken.
7. Close the Ninja Foodi and set seal the valve; using the button "Pressure cook"
8. Set the timer for about 18 minutes and pressure cook at a temperature of about 350°F
9. When the timer beeps; turn off your Ninja Foodi; then do a quick pressure release for 10 minutes
10. Open the lid when it is safe to do; then serve and enjoy your dish!

Nutrition Information

Calories: 269| Fat: 8.3g | Carbohydrates: 24.8g | Fiber: 3.1g |Protein: 5.3g

Recipe 97: Chicken Chettinad

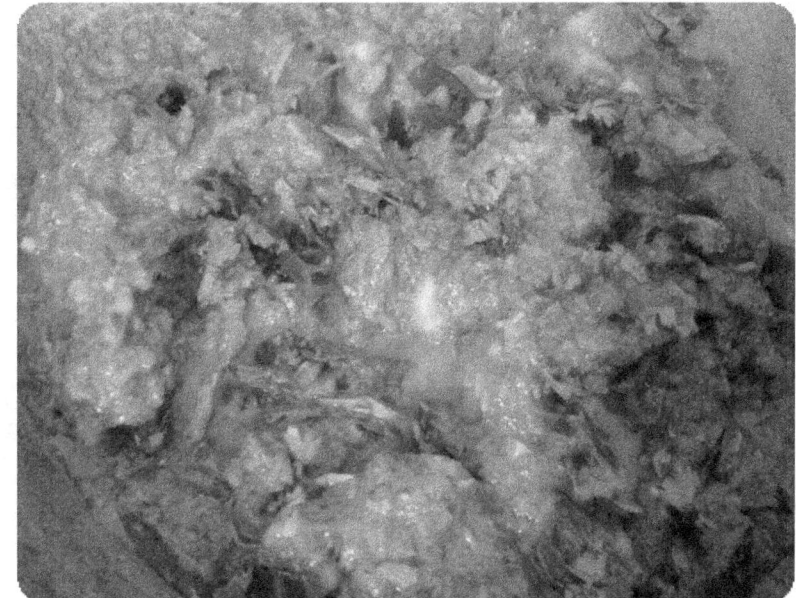

TIME TO PREPARE
10 minutes

COOK TIME
25 Minutes

SERVING
4 People

Ingredients

- 1 teaspoon of ground pepper corns
- 1 teaspoon of coriander powder.
- 3 Cloves of garlic.
- 2 sticks of cinnamon
- ½ lb of chicken
- 2 pieces of cardamom.
- 4 grams of cumin.
- 1tbsp of cumin powder
- 2 curry leaves
- 2 teaspoon of red chilli powder.
- 1 large onion.
- 2tbsp of oil.
- 1tbsp of mustard.
- 3 chillies
- 3 green peppers.
- 1 pinch of ginger
- 1 pinch of fresh and

Instructions

1. Start by heating the oil in a deep pan.
2. Add the mustard, the cumin, the onions, the turmeric, the ginger, the curry leaves and the green chili then sauté the mixture for a few minutes.
3. Now add the tomatoes.
4. Add the coriander and the cumin powder then keep stirring.
5. Add the salt.
6. Preheat your Ninja Foodi to 360° F.
7. Meanwhile, prepare your chicken by coating it with oil, salt and pepper with a pinch of rosemary (Optional).
8. Place the chicken I the Ninja Foodi pressure cook insert
9. Set the timer to about 25 minutes and the pressure to High by pressing the setting function "Pressure cook"
10. Once the timer goes off, set the chicken aside
11. Add the ground black pepper to the mixture you have prepared.
12. Place your chicken in a dish and pour the sauce

chopped coriander
- 2 tomatoes.
- 1+ ½ teaspoon of salt.

around it.

13. Enjoy a well- seasoned chicken Chettinad dish!

Nutrition Information

Calories: 300| Fat: 5g | Carbohydrates: 38g | Fiber: 17g |Protein: 26g

Recipe 98: Ninja Foodi Whole Turkey

TIME TO PREPARE
10 minutes

COOK TIME
35 Minutes

SERVING
5 People

Ingredients

- 1 Whole medium turkey (make sure it fits the air fryer, Around 8lb)
- 6 Tbsp of butter
- 4 Cups of warm water
- 3 tbsp of chicken bouillon
- 2 tbsp of dried parsley
- 2 tbsp of dried and minced onion

Instructions

1. Preheat your Ninja Foodi to a temperature of about 350 ° F.
2. Rinse your turkey and wash it very well.
3. Discard the turkey's giblets.
4. Now, place the turkey in a pan
5. Separate the skin of the turkey in the area of the breast so that you make small pockets.
6. Pour the water and the bouillon in a pan over a medium high heat and season the water with curcuma and salt
7. Add the turkey to the boiling water and cook for about 15 minutes
8. Brush 3 tbsp of butter on both the sides of the turkey and between its skin and the breast meat. (This is meant to make the breast juicy)
9. Add the parsley and the minced onion.
10. Pour the ingredients on the turkey.
11. Add the salt to the turkey.
12. Now, cover the turkey with a foil and place it the Air Crisp Basket of your Ninja Foodi
13. Press the button "Air Crisp" and set the timer to 20

14. When the timer beeps; remove the foil and cook for 5 additional minutes
15. Serve and enjoy the turkey with fried potatoes and salads.

Nutrition Information

Calories: 214| Fat: 8.4g | Carbohydrates: 0.1 g | Fiber: 0g |Protein: 32g

Recipe 99: Chicken Kebabs

TIME TO PREPARE
8 minutes

COOK TIME
18 Minutes

SERVING
6-7 People

Ingredients

- 2 Boneless chicken breasts, cut into pieces of about 2 inches each
- 1 Zucchini, sliced into slices of about 1 inch each
- 1 Red, finely sliced onion
- ½ Pint of grape tomatoes
- 1 tbsp of minced garlic
- 2 tbsp of red wine vinegar
- 1 Juiced lemon
- 1 tsp of oregano
- ¼ cup of olive oil
- 1 Pinch of salt
- 1 Pinch of pepper

Instructions

1. Put the diced chicken into a large bowl. In a separate bowl; place the garlic, the red wine vinegar, the lemon juice; the oregano and the olive oil
2. Pour over the chicken; then toss very well to coat
3. Marinate the chicken for about 15 minutes
4. When you are ready to cook; cut the vegetables in a large bowl; then toss with 1 tbsp of olive oil and sprinkle with some salt and some pepper
5. Measure some skewers to ensure they have the right length to fit in your Air Crisp basket
6. You can cut or break the skewers to fit your Ninja Foodi basket
7. Use the skewers and alternate 1 piece of chicken, a zucchini, a piece of tomato; then add the onion pieces until your ingredients are used
8. Place the chicken kebabs in your Ninja Foodi Basket at a temperature of about 380°F for about 15 to 18 minutes
9. Serve and enjoy your dish!

Nutrition Information

Calories: 143| Fat: 5.9g | Carbohydrates: 7.1 g | Fiber: 0g |Protein: 15.7g

Recipe 100: Chicken Patties

TIME TO PREPARE
10 minutes

COOK TIME
20 Minutes

SERVING
8-9 People

Ingredients

- 1 Pound of lean ground chicken
- ½ Teaspoon of garlic powder
- ½ Tcaspoon of freshly ground black pepper
- 1 Teaspoon of dried sage
- 1 Teaspoon of crushed red pepper flakes
- 1 Teaspoon of dried oregano
- 1 Pinch of Kosher salt

Instructions

1. Preheat your Ninja Foodi air fryer to about 350° F
2. Combine your ingredients altogether into a large bowl; then make sausage patties to your desired thickness and size.
3. Arrange the patties in the Air Crisp basket of your Ninja Foodi and close the lid
4. Press the button Air Crisp and set the timer to about 10
5. Once the timer beeps, remove the patties from the Ninja Foodi
6. Serve and enjoy your delicious chicken patties!

Nutrition Information

Calories: 140| Fat: 11g | Carbohydrates: 2 g | Fiber: 0g |Protein: 15g

CONCLUSION

"The Ninja Foodi Pressure Cooker Cookbook"

This cook book tried to offer you a large array of recipes using a new cooking appliance; the revolutionary Ninja Foodi, which combines pressure cookers, Air Fryers, Ovens and Dehydrator at the same time. And if you haven't heard about the Ninja Foodi, you should start reading this book, because not only will it offer some of the most sumptuous recipes that you can ever stumble into, but it will also offer you useful information that will help you understand the function of this new cooking appliance. So if you are a Newbie in the use of Ninja Foodies, don't get frustrated, because in this book, you will just find everything you need and enough information that will help you understand this cooking appliance better.

So, if you have made your purchase of Ninja Foodi lately; you shouldn't be afraid, because with the help of this book; you will be able to master the use of this revolutionary cooking appliance. Besides; this book will offer you some of the most important tips that may help you using Ninja Foodies perfectly from the first use.

Thereby, with the introduction of Ninja Pressure cookers to your Kitchen and world; you can discover yourself a culinary revolution that has affected the various Kitchen gadgets with the unique cooking appliance, Ninja Pressure Cookers. Ninja Foodi has, indeed, been considered as a more impressive kitchen appliance that many conventional cooking gadgets and appliances. And all the people who have tried using Ninja Foodies find it more impressive and very easy to use. And what most of the people like about the Ninja Foodi is that it can act as an air Fryer, a pressure cooker, a roaster, a slow cooker, a steamer, a dehydrator and more.

So, if you are looking for a unique cooking appliance that can save your money as you will give up on purchasing many cooking appliances at once; this cookbook is the perfect choice for you. And in this book; you will find 200 recipes that vary from breakfast recipes to snacks, appetizers, poultry and different types of meats as well as breads, desserts and different staple recipes.

And what makes this book more special is that you will be able to turn out any type of ingredients into the dish you want in a very short time and you will still get the same delicious taste you are looking for with the simplest ingredients. And whether you want a crispy recipe; a tender one; a roasted taste; you will be able to get it all.

And if you have any doubts about this cooking appliance because it is new and you don't have so much information about it; all you have to do is to download your copy of this book right away because it will clear out any types of ambiguity you have. Get ready to read this book because it will offer you a mixture of everything you need to learn about Ninja Foodies, its benefits, use and more.

Thank you for Reading "the Ninja Foodi Pressure Cooker Cookbook"

We are ecstatic to offer you this Ninja Foodi, Electric Pressure Cooker and Air Fryer cookbook and we hope that you enjoyed it. Please, don't hesitate to share this cookbook with your friends or to whomever you care about. We care about you and your health and we have tried to offer you an exciting cooking journey. And our dear readers; remember that we are always looking forward to any suggestions that will help us continue our work.

www.ingramcontent.com/pod-product-compliance
Lightning Source LLC
Chambersburg PA
CBHW081345070526
44578CB00005B/727